Shane Osborn

appetizers

RECIPES FOR FIRST COURSE OR MAIN EVENT

Shane Osborn
appetizers

RECIPES FOR FIRST COURSE OR MAIN EVENT

photographs by David Loftus

notes

- Ovens and broilers must be preheated to the setting specified in the recipe.
- All cup and spoon measures are level unless otherwise stated.
- Use fresh herbs unless dried herbs are suggested.
- Use sea salt and freshly ground black pepper unless otherwise stated.
- Large eggs should be used except where a different size is specified. Free-range eggs are recommended. Note that a few recipes, including mayonnaise, contain raw or lightly cooked eggs. The young, elderly, pregnant women, and anyone with an immune-deficiency disease should avoid these, because of the slight risk of salmonella.

Publishing director Jane O'Shea   **Project editors** Janet Illsley and Norma MacMillan   **Art director** Vanessa Courtier   **Photographer** David Loftus
Food stylist Shane Osborn   **Production** Beverley Richardson

This edition first published in 2008 by Quadrille Publishing   Text © 2004 Shane Osborn   Photography © 2004 David Loftus
Design and layout © 2004 Quadrille Publishing Limited

ISBN 978 1 84400 639 7   Printed in South China

Library of Congress Cataloging-in-Publication Data
Osborn, Shane, chef.
  Shane Osborn's appetizers : recipes for first course or main event /
photographs by David Loftus.
    p. cm.
  Includes index.
  ISBN 978-1-84400-639-7 (pbk. : lg. print)
  1. Appetizers. 2. Large type books. I. Title. II. Title: Appetizers.
  TX740.O83 2008
  641.812--dc22
                                    2008009780

Contents

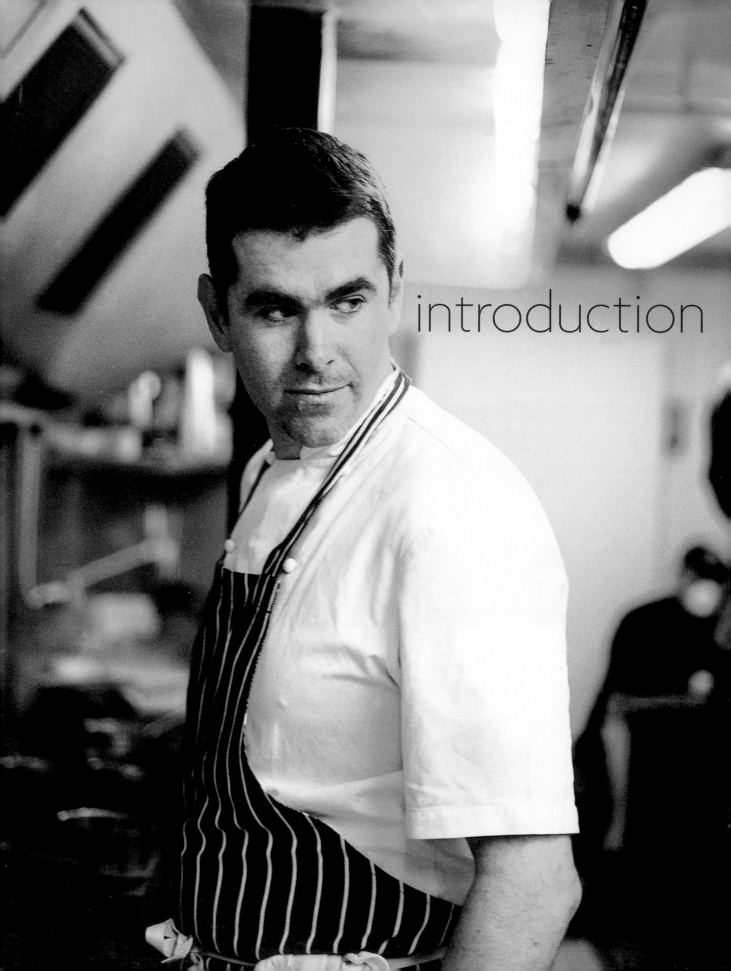

introduction

For me, cooking is about sharing my enjoyment of good food with others. When I say good food, it doesn't have to be gastronomic delights using luxury ingredients. It can be simple food using good fresh produce. Sometimes friends are intimidated when they cook a meal for me, but the one thing all chefs love is to be cooked for. I appreciate all styles of food—seeing and tasting different interpretations of dishes gives me a greater understanding of what customers want to eat.

Although my mother worked as a cook, we never ate extravagantly at home in Australia, just simple, tasty food—homemade hamburgers, lasagnas, and casseroles, for example—humble dishes made well. My first experience of working in a kitchen was part-time at the age of thirteen, doing all sorts of jobs, from peeling vegetables and eggs to dishwashing. I began to realize that cooking really excited me, and at the age of fifteen I started a four-year chef's apprenticeship in Perth.

The things I remember most about the kitchen were the wonderful smells, colors, and textures of the food. School for me was boring and irrelevant, but working in a kitchen was a dream, because I was surrounded by food and I loved eating. I remember scoffing handfuls of chocolate from huge bags in the dry stores, always out of the executive chef's view. I was astonished at the wealth of information and foodie stories my senior chefs would relate, most of them originating from France, Britain, or Spain. The food in Perth in the late 80s had a French influence, something that gave me a curiosity for France—its culture, language, and way of life. In 1991, I decided to go to Europe to see for myself. I was amazed by the fresh produce—salads, herbs, fish, and other ingredients that I had never heard of. I arrived in London thinking I was an experienced chef, but soon realized that there is always something new to learn.

I love experimenting with different ingredients and flavor combinations. "Starters" was a natural choice for my first cookbook, because at the start of a meal appetites are at their keenest and most receptive to new taste experiences. You will find that many of my recipes, especially those in the first three chapters, are surprisingly simple, but they do rely on top quality ingredients, so shop well. The recipes in "Food for groups" are ideal if you are having a party—just increase the quantities to match the number of guests. "Posh" starters are perfect for smaller gatherings and some—but by no means all—of these are a little more challenging. But don't think of the dishes solely as starters. The recipes are versatile and throughout the book you'll find suggestions for serving them as main courses.

Nothing gives me more pleasure than to see and hear the enjoyment my cooking gives customers and friends. Food is a great catalyst for conversation and it provides lasting memories of travel, people, and childhood. It is something that I will always appreciate and I would love everyone to derive as much pleasure from cooking and eating as I do.

nibbles & snacks

Pickled baby vegetables

Vegetable crisps

Home-roasted nuts with herbs & sea salt

Crisp marinated quail eggs

Curried quail eggs

Button mushroom beignets

Leek & red onion tartlets

Sweet onion & anchovy pastries

Herb-crusted tuna with olive & shallot dressing

Smoked eel pâté with apple & lime

Smoked salmon with horseradish mousse

Sautéed chicken livers on garlic croûtes

Roasted new potatoes wrapped in prosciutto

Foie gras parfait with poppy seed crisps

Pickled baby vegetables

SERVES 8–10

marinade

¼ cup olive oil

*4oz shallots, peeled and
    thinly sliced*

3 garlic cloves, peeled

1 tbsp sea salt

5 white peppercorns

10 coriander seeds

½oz thyme sprigs

2 bay leaves

1¼ cups white wine vinegar

vegetables

10 baby globe artichokes

20 baby carrots

½ small head cauliflower

20 baby onions

10 baby eggplants

*7oz chanterelles or other
    mushrooms*

marinade   Heat the olive oil in a medium pan over a low heat. Add the shallots, garlic, salt, peppercorns, coriander seeds, thyme, and bay leaves. Stir, then cover and sweat gently, stirring occasionally, until the shallots are soft, 10–12 minutes. Add the wine vinegar and reduce until almost dry, then add 2½ cups water and bring to a boil. Lower the heat and let simmer for 15 minutes.

preparing the vegetables   Halve or quarter the artichokes; peel and trim the carrots; cut the cauliflower into tiny florets; peel the baby onions; slice the eggplants; trim and clean the mushrooms.

pickling the vegetables   Cook each type of vegetable separately. Add to the marinade and simmer gently until just tender, 5–10 minutes; test by piercing with a small, sharp knife. Return all the vegetables to the pickling marinade and let cool. When cool, the vegetables are ready to serve. (Alternatively, they can be kept chilled in the marinade for up to 1 week.) Strain and reserve the liquid, as it can be used to pickle another batch of vegetables; it will keep in the fridge for up to 1 week.

to serve   Drain the vegetables and arrange in small bowls or on platters to serve as canapés.

note   These pickled baby vegetables have many uses. In the restaurant we serve them as nibbles, garnishes, main course accompaniments, and salads, partnered with interesting leaves and herbs. As an accompaniment, pickled cauliflower cuts the richness of salmon and tuna beautifully. In a similar way, the sweet acidity of pickled artichokes is the perfect foil for foie gras and rich terrines.

as a salad starter

Toss the pickled vegetables with a selection of salad leaves, such as arugula, baby chard, and young sorrel or spinach. Add wafer-thin slices of smoked duck breast (or prosciutto or bresaola), if desired. Drizzle a little extra virgin olive oil over the salad just before serving, if required.

Vegetable crisps

SERVES 10

2 parsnips
1 large sweet potato
2 large beets
3 salsify sticks
8 large Jerusalem artichokes
oil for deep-frying
sea salt
small handful of parsley sprigs

preparing the root vegetables   Peel the vegetables and trim the ends, then cut lengthwise into wafer-thin slices, using a mandoline or swivel vegetable peeler.

deep-frying the crisps   Heat the oil in a deep-fryer or deep, heavy pot to 350°F. Deep-fry the vegetable slices in small batches (a handful at a time) to ensure they cook evenly. Add to the hot oil and deep-fry until they just start to crisp and color lightly, 15–30 seconds. Remove with a slotted spoon and tip onto paper towels to drain. Season the crisps immediately with sea salt, while hot.

to serve   When you have deep-fried all the root vegetables, add the parsley sprigs to the oil and deep-fry until crisp, about 10 seconds; remove and drain on paper towels. Toss the parsley sprigs with the vegetable crisps and serve in bowls.

note   Vegetable crisps are an ideal garnish for main course game dishes.

variations   To vary the flavor, sprinkle the hot crisps sparingly with curry powder, paprika, ground cumin, or mushroom powder.

Home-roasted nuts with herbs & sea salt

SERVES 10

8oz skinned almonds
8oz macadamia nuts
8oz unsalted peanuts
1 tsp chopped thyme
1 tsp chopped rosemary, plus
  sprigs for garnish
sea salt

roasting the nuts   Preheat the oven to 350°F. Scatter the nuts evenly on a baking sheet lined with parchment paper and roast until lightly colored, 6–8 minutes.

to flavor   Tip the roasted nuts into a bowl, then add the chopped herbs and season with sea salt while still hot. Toss to mix and let cool. Serve garnished with rosemary.

variations   Flavor the nuts with spices, such as smoked paprika, cumin seeds, or curry powder, rather than herbs.

Crisp marinated quail eggs

MAKES 12

12 quail eggs
2 tsp white wine vinegar
1 tbsp truffle oil
salt

to finish
oil for deep-frying
1 egg
1 tbsp milk
2 tbsp all-purpose flour
1 cup fresh white bread crumbs
  (preferably a day old)
1 tbsp finely chopped chives

poaching the quail eggs   Do this a day ahead. Using a small, serrated knife, carefully remove one-fourth of the shell from the wider end of each quail egg and tip the egg out into a small bowl containing 1 tsp wine vinegar. When all the eggs are in the bowl, let them stand for 3–4 minutes. Meanwhile, bring a large, deep pan of water (about 2 quarts) to a boil. Add 1 tsp wine vinegar and turn the heat down to a gentle simmer. Stir the water in a circular motion to create a whirlpool, then tip the quail eggs into the center. Poach for 1 minute, then check by scooping out one egg—it should be firm, but spongy. When ready, lift out the eggs with a slotted spoon and place in a bowl of ice water. After 5 minutes, transfer them to a small bowl, using a slotted spoon. Pour the truffle oil over them, cover the bowl tightly with plastic wrap, and let marinate in the fridge overnight.

the next day   Heat the oil in a deep-fryer, or deep, heavy pot, to 350°F. In the meantime, beat the egg with the milk in a small bowl; scatter the flour on a plate; combine the bread crumbs and chives in a small bowl. Using a small slotted spoon, take a marinated quail egg, shaking off excess truffle oil. Roll in the flour, then dip into the egg mix, and, finally, roll in the bread crumbs to coat all over. Deep-fry the eggs in two batches: Immerse in the hot oil and fry until crisp and golden brown, 20–30 seconds. Drain on paper towels, season with salt, and serve while still hot.

Curried quail eggs

MAKES 24

12 quail eggs (at room
  temperature)
1 tsp mayonnaise
pinch of curry powder, to taste
salt

to finish
paprika for sprinkling
12 small cilantro sprigs

boiling the quail eggs   Bring a small pan of water to a boil. Using a spoon, carefully lower the quail eggs into the water. Cook for 2 minutes and 20 seconds. Remove with a slotted spoon to a bowl of ice water.

stuffing the quail eggs   Carefully peel the eggs, then halve lengthwise. Scoop out the yolks and put into a small bowl. Mash the yolks with the mayonnaise, add the curry powder, and season with salt to taste. Spoon the yolk mixture into the whites, using a teaspoon. Sprinkle with paprika and top each stuffed egg with a cilantro sprig.

Button mushroom beignets

SERVES 8–10

beignet mix
1¼ cups milk
½ onion, peeled and roughly diced
3 tarragon sprigs
6 tbsp unsalted butter
2 tbsp all-purpose flour
salt and pepper
1lb button mushrooms, cleaned and finely sliced
2 egg yolks, beaten

batter
1 cup cornstarch (lightly filled)
1 cup all-purpose flour
2 tsp baking powder
1¾ cups sparkling water (approximately)

to finish
oil for deep-frying
flour for dusting

béchamel   Put the milk and onion into a pan and slowly bring to a boil, then take off the heat. Add the tarragon and let infuse for 30 minutes. Strain. Melt 1 tbsp butter in a pan, stir in the flour, and cook, stirring, over a low heat for 2–3 minutes. Gradually stir in the infused milk, keeping the sauce smooth. Cook the béchamel gently for 10 minutes, stirring frequently. Season with a little salt and transfer to a bowl. Cover the surface with damp parchment paper to prevent a skin from forming and let cool.

sautéed mushrooms   Heat half of the remaining butter in a large frying pan and sauté half the mushrooms over a high heat until golden, 3–4 minutes. Season, then tip into a colander to drain and cool. Repeat with the remaining mushrooms. (Cooking in two batches ensures that the mushrooms fry rather than stew.) When cool, work in a food processor until finely diced, 15–20 seconds. Stir into the cooled béchamel; adjust the seasoning. Mix in the egg yolks. Cover and chill for 20 minutes.

shaping the beignets   Spoon the beignet mixture into a pastry bag fitted with a ½-inch plain tip. Pipe in parallel lines onto a baking sheet lined with parchment paper, the full length of the sheet. (Make sure the sheet will fit into your freezer.) Freeze the beignet logs until ready to serve.

batter   Sift the dry ingredients together into a bowl. Gradually whisk in the water, keeping the mixture smooth and stopping when the batter has a coating consistency. Cover and let rest in the fridge for 10 minutes.

to serve   Heat the oil for deep-frying to 350°F. Cut a frozen beignet log into 3-inch-long batons. Dust the batons lightly with flour, then dip in the batter to coat and carefully add to the hot oil. Deep-fry until golden brown, 1–1½ minutes. Using a slotted spoon, remove to a plate lined with paper towels, season, and keep warm. Repeat to cook the rest of the beignets, no more than six at a time. Serve immediately.

as a main course   Use the béchamel and mushrooms as the basis for a pie to serve 4. Sauté 3 skinned, boned, and chopped chicken breast halves in a little butter until golden and just tender, then stir into the béchamel with the sautéed mushrooms. Spoon into a 4-cup baking dish. Brush the rim with water and cover with a sheet of ready-rolled puff pastry. Brush with egg wash and bake at 425°F until golden, 15–20 minutes.

Leek & red onion tartlets

MAKES 10–12

pastry shells

*½ quantity basic short pastry
    (page 156)*

flour for dusting

filling

2 tbsp unsalted butter

*2 red onions, peeled and thinly
    sliced*

*1 large leek, split lengthwise,
    cleaned, and thinly sliced*

1 garlic clove, peeled and smashed

1 tsp chopped sage

salt and pepper

to finish

*12 thin slices of smoked chorizo
    sausage*

tartlet shells   Preheat the oven to 400°F. Dust a work surface lightly with flour and roll out the pastry to ⅛-inch thickness. Cover with plastic wrap and let rest for 30 minutes. Cut out disks and use to line 10–12 tartlet molds, 2½–3 inches in diameter. Prick the bases with a fork and line with parchment paper and baking beans. Cover with plastic wrap and let rest in the fridge for 30 minutes. Remove the plastic wrap and bake the tartlet shells until golden brown and crisp, 15–20 minutes. Transfer to a wire rack to cool slightly, removing the paper and beans.

leek and red onion filling   Melt the butter in a medium pan over a low heat. Add the red onions, leek, garlic, and sage, and season generously with salt and pepper. Stir, then cover and sweat until tender, 10–15 minutes. Drain on paper towels.

to serve   Spoon the warm leek and onion mixture into the tartlet shells. Roll each chorizo slice into a cornet and place on top. Serve warm.

variation   Make the filling as above, then chop the chorizo and stir it in. Brush a sheet of phyllo pastry with melted butter and top with a second phyllo sheet. Spoon the filling along one long edge of the layered pastry. Brush the pastry edges with melted butter and roll up. Place on a baking sheet, tucking the ends underneath, and brush all over with melted butter. Bake at 400°F for 10–12 minutes. Cut the phyllo roll into bite-sized pieces. Serve warm.

Sweet onion & anchovy pastries

MAKES 32

pastry bases

*12oz frozen puff pastry (about
¾ package), thawed*

sweet onion topping

1½ tbsp unsalted butter

*3 large onions, peeled and thinly
sliced*

2 garlic cloves, peeled and crushed

salt

to finish

*about 40 white anchovies in oil,
drained*

2 tbsp olive oil for drizzling

small flat-leaf parsley sprigs

sweet onion topping   Melt the butter in a medium pan. Add the onions, garlic, and a pinch of salt, and fry gently until the onions begin to soften. Turn the heat down to very low and cook, uncovered, for about 40 minutes so the onions caramelize very slowly. Stir from time to time to prevent them from sticking and burning. When ready, they will be deep brown and taste very rich and sweet. Set aside to cool.

pastry bases   Preheat the oven to 425°F. Roll out the pastry to ¼-inch thickness and cut four 8- by 4-inch rectangles. Place these on a large baking sheet lined with parchment paper. Prick the pastry all over with a fork. Spoon the sweet onions onto the pastry bases and spread gently and thinly, leaving a ¼-inch border around the edges. Bake until well risen and golden brown at the edges, 12–15 minutes. Transfer to a wire rack to cool. Turn the oven down to 400°F.

to assemble   Arrange the anchovies on the tarts in a criss-cross fashion. Using a very sharp knife, trim away the two shorter crusts on each tart, including the tips of the anchovies. Cut four paper rectangles, slightly larger than the tarts.

to serve   Place the tarts on a baking sheet. Lay the paper on top, against the skin of the anchovies. Reheat in the oven for 6–8 minutes until the paper is very hot to the touch; don't let it burn. Remove the paper and lift the tarts onto a board. Cut into small squares to serve as a canapé. Drizzle with olive oil, garnish with parsley, and serve warm.

as a starter, lunch, or supper   The beauty of this dish is that it can be upsized easily. For a starter to serve 8, simply halve the rectangular tarts to give larger squares. For a lunch or supper to serve 4–6, make one large rectangular tart. Cut into generous slices and serve with a leafy salad. The cutting of the pastry is flexible and you can intersperse the anchovies with small black olives to vary the topping.

Herb-crusted tuna with olive & shallot dressing

MAKES 20–30

herb-crusted tuna

*14oz fresh center-cut tuna loin,
cut into 1 or 2 long, 1¼-inch
squared logs*

4 white anchovies in oil, drained

salt

3 tbsp olive oil

olive and shallot vinaigrette

*2 large shallots, peeled and finely
diced*

2 tbsp red wine vinegar

10 black olives, pitted and chopped

4 tbsp olive oil

to finish

*1½ cups chopped soft herbs,
such as parsley, basil, chives,
and tarragon*

*small salad leaves, such as
watercress, mâche, and baby
spinach*

olive and shallot vinaigrette   Make this a day ahead, if possible. Put the diced shallots into a small bowl and add the wine vinegar. Cover and let marinate for a few hours, or preferably overnight. Stir in the chopped olives and olive oil. Cover and refrigerate until needed (for up to a week).

herb-crusted tuna   Slit the tuna logs lengthwise through to the center and insert two anchovies in each log, end to end. Press the edges of the tuna together to enclose. Season the surface of the fish all over with salt. Heat a large nonstick frying pan over a high heat, then add the olive oil. When it is almost smoking, add the tuna and sear for 5–8 seconds on each of the four sides. Remove and drain on paper towels, then let rest for 5 minutes. Scatter the chopped herbs on a plate, then roll the tuna logs in the herbs to coat evenly on all sides. Cover and chill for at least 1 hour.

to serve   Using a sharp knife, cut the tuna logs into ¾-inch slices and arrange on cold plates. Spoon the marinated vinaigrette over the tuna and scatter small salad leaves around the plates. Serve at room temperature, within an hour of assembling.

as a main course   This recipe lends itself easily to upsizing. For a main dish, double the quantities and ask the fishmonger for thicker pieces of tuna loin, ideally 2-inch squared logs. Sear for a little longer, 10–15 seconds on each side. Continue as above. Serve the sliced tuna with assorted salad leaves, dressed simply with olive oil, lemon juice, salt, and pepper. Drizzle the shallot and olive vinaigrette over the plates. Crushed fingerling potatoes flavored with chives would be a perfect accompaniment.

Smoked eel pâté with apple & lime

MAKES 16

pâté

5oz smoked eel fillet (or smoked mackerel)
5 tbsp unsalted butter, softened
salt and pepper
juice of ½ lime

for serving

2–3 thin slices of white bread
1 Granny Smith apple
1 lime

smoked eel pâté   Put the fish into a food processor and process briefly to a paste, about 30 seconds. Add the softened butter and process again until smooth, about 30 seconds. Transfer the mixture to a bowl. Season with salt and pepper, and add half the lime juice, to taste. (Reserve the rest of the lime juice for the apple.)

melba toast   Preheat the oven to 375°F. Heat the broiler (unless you prefer to use the toaster). Toast the bread slices until lightly colored on both sides. Cool slightly, then remove the crusts and cut each slice horizontally in half. Rub with your fingers to remove loose crumbs. Cut into quarters, then halve each toast to make wafer-thin triangles. Place on a baking sheet. Leave in a warm place for 10 minutes to curl, then bake until crisp, about 10 minutes. Let cool.

to serve   Peel, halve, and core the apple. Cut into very thin slices and toss in the reserved lime juice to prevent discoloration. Peel the lime, removing all pith, then cut the sections from the membrane. Place a generous spoonful of fish pâté on each melba toast triangle and top with an apple slice and a lime section.

note   This pâté makes an excellent sandwich filling. Split a crusty baguette lengthwise, spread with the smoked eel pâté, and top with slices of tomato and ripe avocado. Put the bread back together and serve.

Smoked salmon with horseradish mousse

Illustrated on page 24

MAKES 35–40

1lb thinly sliced smoked salmon

horseradish mousse

$2/3$ cup heavy cream, chilled

*2 tbsp freshly grated horseradish
   or 3 tbsp hot horseradish sauce*

squeeze of lemon juice

salt and pepper

for serving

pumpernickel or rye bread

lemon wedges (optional)

horseradish mousse   Put a mixing bowl in the freezer to chill thoroughly. Whip the cream in the chilled bowl until it just starts to thicken, then add the horseradish and a squeeze of lemon juice. Whip a little more until thick, but not stiff. Add a pinch of salt and several grinds of pepper, then set aside to infuse for 15 minutes. Finish by whipping the cream until it is just stiff. Put into a pastry bag fitted with a $1/2$-inch plain tip and refrigerate until well chilled, about 20 minutes.

smoked salmon rolls   Cut the smoked salmon slices into rectangles 3–4 inches wide and 6–8 inches long. Tear off a sheet of plastic wrap that is slightly longer than a salmon rectangle. Lay the rectangle horizontally on the wrap, leaving at least $1^{1/4}$ inches of wrap free at the front. Pipe a line of horseradish mousse along the salmon, $3/4$ inch from the edge closest to you. Lift the wrap overhang and roll the salmon around the horseradish mousse to enclose it and form a sausage shape. Twist the ends of the wrap tightly and tie to seal, then place in the freezer. Repeat with the rest of the salmon and horseradish mousse.

to serve   Unwrap the frozen salmon rolls and cut into $1/2$-inch slices. Thaw at room temperature for about 30 minutes. Serve on squares of pumpernickel or rye bread, with lemon wedges if desired.

as a starter   *Illustrated on page 25*

Take a large slice of smoked salmon and put a generous spoonful of horseradish mousse on one side. Bring the other half of the salmon over the mousse to enclose it, then flip over and trim the edges to neaten, if desired. Serve with rye or pumpernickel bread and lemon wedges.

Sautéed chicken livers on garlic croûtes

MAKES 12

garlic croûtes
12 slices of baguette
4 tbsp unsalted butter, melted
2 garlic cloves, peeled and halved

sautéed chicken livers
4oz chicken livers, trimmed
1 tbsp peanut oil
1 onion, peeled and finely diced
splash of red wine vinegar
salt and pepper

for serving
½ tsp chopped thyme
garlic crisps (page 62), optional

garlic croûtes   Preheat the broiler. Brush the baguette slices with the butter and rub with a little garlic. Toast on both sides under the hot broiler (while you sauté the chicken livers).

sautéed chicken livers   Rinse the chicken livers and pat dry with paper towels, then chop roughly and set aside. Heat the oil in a nonstick sauté pan over a low heat, then add the diced onion. Cover and sweat until softened, 5–7 minutes. Increase the heat and add the chicken livers. Sauté, stirring, over a high heat for 1½ minutes. Add the wine vinegar and season with salt and pepper to taste.

to serve   Spoon the chicken liver mixture onto the warm garlic croûtes and sprinkle with chopped thyme. Scatter a few garlic crisps on top of each one, if desired.

note   These sautéed chicken livers are delicious served for brunch on a bed of salad leaves lightly dressed with vinaigrette. Accompany with toasted brioche slices and pear chutney (page 157).

Roasted new potatoes wrapped in prosciutto

MAKES 24

24 Yukon Gold potatoes or other
small, waxy potatoes

3 garlic cloves, peeled and crushed

3 rosemary sprigs

1 chicken bouillon cube, crumbled

salt

12 long slices of prosciutto or
Serrano ham, halved

avocado crème fraîche

1 ripe avocado

2–3 tbsp crème fraîche

squeeze of lemon juice

for serving

2 tbsp olive oil

cracked black pepper

sea salt

parboiling the potatoes   Put the potatoes in a saucepan and cover with cold water. Add the garlic, rosemary, chicken bouillon cube, and a pinch of salt. Bring to a simmer and cook gently until the potatoes are just tender, 15–20 minutes.

roasting the potatoes   Preheat the oven to 400°F. Drain the potatoes thoroughly. Wrap each potato tightly in a half-slice of prosciutto, then place on a baking sheet. Bake until the prosciutto is lightly caramelized, 6–8 minutes. The prosciutto will shrink in the oven to form a tight wrap around the potatoes. Let cool slightly.

avocado crème fraîche   Prepare this while the potatoes are in the oven. Peel, halve, and pit the avocado, then roughly chop the flesh. Put into a blender with 2 tsp cold water and blend until smooth. Transfer to a bowl and fold in the crème fraîche. Add the lemon juice and season with salt to taste.

to serve   Using a sharp knife, cut the prosciutto-wrapped potatoes into chunky slices, or simply cut them in half. Arrange on a platter, drizzle the olive oil over, and sprinkle with cracked black pepper and sea salt. Provide toothpicks and serve the avocado crème fraîche as a dip.

note   If you prepare the avocado crème fraîche in advance, cover it with plastic wrap, pressing the wrap onto the surface of the avocado mixture, and refrigerate. The wrap helps to prevent discoloration.

as a starter or main course   Use
the prosciutto-wrapped potatoes as the basis for a
warm salad. Toss the sliced potatoes with a few
handfuls of baby sorrel or spinach leaves and a
sliced avocado. Drizzle with vinaigrette.

Foie gras parfait with poppy seed crisps

MAKES 24–30

parfait

*4oz chicken livers, trimmed and
roughly chopped*

*4oz foie gras, trimmed and
roughly chopped*

3 eggs, beaten

1/2 cup port wine

1/2 cup Madeira

1 shallot, peeled and minced

1 bay leaf

1 thyme sprig

14 tbsp butter, melted (1 3/4 cups)

salt and pepper

poppy seed crisps

2 sheets phyllo pastry

4 tbsp unsalted butter, melted

1 tsp poppy seeds

foie gras parfait   Take the chicken livers, foie gras, and eggs out of the fridge an hour ahead to bring to room temperature. Preheat the oven to 325°F. Put the port, Madeira, shallot, bay leaf, and thyme into a pan and bring to a boil. Let bubble until reduced by two-thirds, then remove from the heat and discard the herbs; let cool slightly. Meanwhile, gently warm the chicken livers and foie gras in a pan over a low heat until lukewarm, 30–45 seconds. Tip into a blender, add the reduced liquid and eggs, and blend until smooth. With the motor running, slowly add the melted butter and blend for 2 minutes. Season with 1/2 tsp salt and 6 turns of the pepper mill. Pass through a fine sieve into a bowl.

cooking the parfait   Spoon the parfait mixture into a greased medium-sized soufflé dish. Set in a shallow roasting pan and surround with warm water to come halfway up the sides. Bake until just firm on the surface, 35–45 minutes. Remove from the oven and let cool in the pan of water, then take out, cover, and refrigerate.

poppy seed crisps   Increase the oven temperature to 400°F. Lay the phyllo sheets on a baking sheet lined with parchment paper. Brush with the melted butter and sprinkle with the poppy seeds and salt. Bake until golden, about 8 minutes. Transfer to a wire rack to cool.

to serve   Break the phylo pastry into irregular pieces. Spoon or pipe a small mound of parfait on half of the poppy seed crisps. Top each one with another phyllo crisp and serve.

note   This parfait is also excellent as a starter, with toasted brioche or walnut bread, cornichons, and a chutney, such as pear chutney (page 157).

quick & easy

Cèpe, artichoke & fava bean salad

Eggplant roasted couscous

Corn fritters with crisp bacon & soft cheese

Minestrone

Roasted spring carrots with star anise & tarragon

Roasted goat cheese & red pepper salad

Soft polenta with gruyère & mushroom fricassée

Scallops with basil oil & crisp serrano ham

Oysters with shallot vinaigrette & watercress

Mussels in a creamy sauce with basil

Mackerel with sweet & sour pepper jus

Sardine frittata with green onions

Roasted skate wing with crispy capers

Seared salmon with cauliflower purée

Poached cod with chive scrambled eggs

Warm chicken, baby spinach & mozzarella salad

Warm salad of arugula & lamb with garlic crisps

Cèpe, artichoke & fava bean salad

SERVES 4

2 large globe artichokes

*1 quantity pickling marinade
(see page 10)*

4oz shelled fresh fava beans

*10oz fresh cèpes or shiitake
mushrooms*

2 tbsp olive oil

1 shallot, peeled and finely diced

salt

mushroom and thyme vinaigrette

1¼ cups olive oil

*1½ cups roughly chopped shiitake
mushrooms*

1 garlic clove, peeled

3–4 thyme sprigs

salt

½ shallot, peeled and minced

7 tbsp balsamic vinegar

to finish

*3 cups arugula or baby spinach
leaves*

1 tbsp olive oil

1 tsp balsamic vinegar

mushroom and thyme vinaigrette   Make this in advance. Heat a small frying pan over a high heat, then add 2 tbsp olive oil. When hot, add the mushrooms, garlic, thyme, and a pinch of salt. Cook, stirring occasionally, until the mushrooms are browned, 4–5 minutes. Add the shallot and cook over a low heat until the shallot is lightly browned, 1–2 minutes. Take the pan off the heat and add the balsamic vinegar to deglaze, scraping up the sediment on the bottom of the pan. Tip the mixture into a blender or food processor, add the remaining olive oil, and blend until smooth, about 1 minute. Pour into a jar and let cool, then cover tightly and refrigerate until needed.

artichokes   Pull off the outer leaves from the artichokes to reveal the fleshy bottoms or hearts. Trim well and remove the hairy choke. Bring the pickling marinade to a simmer in a pan, add the artichoke hearts, and simmer until just tender, about 5 minutes. Remove from the heat and let cool in the marinade.

fava beans   Add the fava beans to a pan of boiling salted water and blanch until tender, 1½–2 minutes. Drain and immediately refresh in ice water. Drain and slip the fava beans out of their skins.

to assemble   Cut the cooked artichoke hearts into ³/₄-inch dice. Cut the cèpes or shiitake mushrooms into ¼-inch-thick slices. Heat a nonstick pan over a high heat and add the 2 tbsp olive oil. When hot, add the artichokes and mushrooms, season with salt, and sauté until light brown in color, 2–3 minutes. Remove from the heat and add the finely diced shallot and fava beans. Toss to mix. Leave in the pan for 2 minutes to warm through.

to serve   Dress the salad leaves with the olive oil and balsamic vinegar. Pile the warm artichoke and mushroom salad on warmed plates and drizzle the mushroom and thyme vinaigrette over. Top with the salad leaves.

Eggplant roasted couscous

SERVES 6

1 eggplant, about 1¼lb

½ cup olive oil

2 tsp ground cumin

1⅓ cups quick-cooking couscous

3 garlic cloves, peeled and crushed

1¼ cups hot chicken stock
   (page 156)

2 tomatoes, peeled, seeded, and
   roughly chopped

15 basil leaves, shredded

salt and pepper

4 large basil leaves, deep-fried
   if desired, for garnish

preparing the eggplant   Peel the eggplant, then cut the flesh into ½-inch cubes. Heat a large, heavy-based frying pan over a high heat and add 3 tbsp of the olive oil. When hot, add the eggplant cubes and cumin. Fry, stirring frequently, until the eggplant is golden brown and tender, 2–3 minutes. Remove with a slotted spoon and drain on paper towels.

pan-roasting the couscous   Reheat the pan, then add the rest of the olive oil. When very hot, add the couscous with the garlic and fry, turning frequently, until golden brown, 2–3 minutes.

to assemble   Add the stock to the couscous, along with the eggplant cubes, tomatoes, and shredded basil. Toss to mix, then remove from the heat and cover tightly. Let stand for 5 minutes.

to serve   Uncover and fork through the couscous. Taste and adjust the seasoning. Divide the couscous among warmed plates or bowls and garnish with deep-fried or fresh basil leaves. Serve at once.

as a main course   Season 4 lamb sirloin chops and cook on an oiled grill pan or outdoor grill until well browned, but still pink inside, 4–5 minutes on each side. Serve with the warm eggplant roasted couscous.

Corn fritters with crisp bacon & soft cheese

SERVES 4

corn fritters
2/3 cup all-purpose flour
2 tsp baking powder
1/2 cup milk
2 tbsp drained canned corn
pinch of salt
2 tbsp vegetable oil for frying

to assemble
8 slices of bacon
4oz soft goat cheese

corn fritter batter   Sift the flour and baking powder together into a bowl, make a well in the middle, and add the milk, corn, and salt. Whisk together until evenly blended, then cover and let rest for 15 minutes.

oven-crisped bacon   Preheat the oven to 425°F. Lay the bacon slices side by side on a sturdy baking sheet. Place another heavy baking sheet on top to keep them flat and cook in the oven until crisp, 8–12 minutes. Drain on paper towels.

to cook the fritters   Heat a large nonstick frying pan over a medium heat and add the vegetable oil. When hot, cook the fritters: Spoon in 2 tbsp batter for each fritter, spacing them well apart. Fry until golden underneath, 1–2 minutes, then carefully turn over, using a spatula, and cook the other side until brown and crisp, 1–2 minutes. Drain on paper towels.

to serve   Cut each corn fritter in half and arrange on serving plates with a spoonful of soft goat cheese. Top with the crisp bacon slices.

as a main course Omit the bacon and cheese. Double the batter quantity and cook larger fritters (4 tbsp batter for each). Flatten 8 chicken thighs and fry, skin-side down, in a little oil for 8–10 minutes, then turn and fry until cooked through, 2–3 minutes longer. Heat 1 cup corn kernels with 1 cup chicken stock for 3 minutes, then purée in a blender and pass through a sieve. Serve the chicken thighs on the corn fritters with the corn purée and a watercress salad.

Minestrone

SERVES 4

1 tbsp olive oil
1 garlic clove, peeled
2 tbsp diced onion
1/2 cup diced leek
1/2 cup diced carrot
1/2 cup diced celery
2 thyme sprigs
2 bay leaves
salt and pepper
2 tsp tomato paste
2/3 cup peeled and diced potato,
*   rinsed*
20 strands of spaghetti,
*   broken into 3/4-inch lengths*
2 tomatoes, seeded and diced
8 basil leaves, chopped

basil oil
1/2 cup basil leaves
1/4 cup olive oil

minestrone   Heat the olive oil in a medium pan with the garlic clove. Add the onion, leek, carrot, and celery, along with the thyme, bay leaves, and a pinch of salt. Stir, then cover and sweat over a low heat until the vegetables have softened, 5–6 minutes. Add the tomato paste, potato, and 4 cups water. Bring to a boil, then add the pasta. Bring back to a simmer and skim the surface, then simmer gently until the potato and pasta are cooked, 10–12 minutes. Discard the garlic clove.

basil oil   While the soup is simmering, blanch the basil leaves in boiling salted water for 25 seconds; drain well. Blend the basil in a blender with the olive oil until smooth, 30–40 seconds.

to finish   Stir the diced tomatoes and chopped basil into the soup, then taste and adjust the seasoning. Ladle into warmed deep bowls and sprinkle with the basil oil. Serve immediately.

note   For a simple finish, omit the basil oil and serve the minestrone sprinkled with freshly grated Parmesan and small basil leaves. To make the soup more substantial replace the spaghetti with a large handful of penne, and serve each portion topped with some cheesy croûtons.

Roasted spring carrots with star anise & tarragon

SERVES 4

1¼lb baby spring carrots or other
   thin, small carrots
3 tbsp unsalted butter
4 star anise
salt and pepper
large pinch of sugar
½ cup chicken stock or vegetable
   nage (page 156)
¼ cup tarragon leaves, roughly
   torn

pan-roasting the carrots   Peel the carrots and trim them down to an even size, leaving on a tuft of the green stem. Place a large nonstick frying pan over a medium heat. When hot, add the butter along with the star anise. As soon as the butter starts foaming, add the carrots and season with salt. Let the carrots roast slowly in the butter for 7–8 minutes, rolling them from time to time to ensure they turn golden on all sides.

caramelizing the carrots   Drain off the excess butter from the pan, then sprinkle the sugar over the carrots and turn for a few moments to glaze on all sides. Pour in the stock and let bubble slowly until it is reduced down to a sticky aromatic glaze and the carrots are just cooked—they should retain a slight bite.

to finish   Scatter the torn tarragon leaves over the carrots and check the seasoning. Divide the carrots among warmed plates and drizzle with a little of the glaze. Retain the star anise as a garnish. Serve at once.

note   If the glaze is too sticky, thin with a little hot stock or water before spooning over the carrots to serve.

as a main course   Season 2 small pork tenderloins and brown in a little oil in a frying pan over a high heat. Transfer to a roasting pan and roast at 400°F until cooked through, 15–20 minutes. Remove from the oven and let rest for 10 minutes. Meanwhile, cook 12 baby turnips in boiling salted water until tender, 7–8 minutes; drain and toss with butter. Halve the pork tenderloins and serve on the roasted carrots with the turnips and glaze.

Roasted goat cheese & red pepper salad

SERVES 4

roasted peppers

2 red bell peppers

2 tbsp olive oil

salt and pepper

roasted goat cheese

2 tsp chopped walnuts

2 tsp chopped hazelnuts

4 tbsp bread crumbs

2 egg yolks

1 tbsp milk

4 slices firm goat cheese log or
*   4 small whole cheeses, about*
*   2½oz each*

2 tbsp all-purpose flour for dusting

for serving

20 black olives, pitted

4oz mixed salad leaves, such as
*   frisée, mâche, and radicchio*

2 tbsp vinaigrette (page 157)

roasting the peppers   Preheat the oven to 425°F. Cut the red peppers in half and remove the seeds and white membrane. Brush all over with olive oil, season with salt and pepper, and place on a baking sheet. Roast until softened and lightly colored, 15–20 minutes. Let cool.

roasting the goat cheese   Combine the chopped nuts with the bread crumbs on a plate. Beat the egg yolks with the milk (to make an egg wash). Dust the slices of goat cheese with flour to coat lightly. One at a time, dip the slices into the egg wash, then into the crumb-nut mixture to coat evenly all over. Place the crumb-coated cheese slices on a baking sheet lined with parchment paper. Bake, turning once or twice, until the coating is crisp and golden brown, 6–8 minutes.

to serve   Cut each roasted pepper half into quarters and arrange on warmed plates with the roasted goat cheese and olives. Dress the salad leaves with vinaigrette, season, and pile alongside.

Soft polenta with gruyère & mushroom fricassée

SERVES 4

polenta

2 cups chicken stock or vegetable nage (page 156)

salt and pepper

1 heaped cup polenta (yellow cornmeal)

3 tbsp unsalted butter

1 cup shredded Gruyère cheese, plus extra for serving

mushroom fricassée

5oz wild mushrooms, cleaned and trimmed

2 tbsp olive oil

2 garlic cloves, peeled and cracked

1 tbsp chopped parsley

squeeze of lemon juice, to taste

to cook the polenta   Bring the stock to a boil in a large saucepan and add a large pinch of salt. Slowly pour in the polenta (cornmeal), whisking constantly as you do so to prevent lumps from forming. Cook the polenta over a low heat, stirring frequently, until the stock is absorbed and the mixture is very thick, 15–20 minutes.

mushroom fricassée   Halve or slice any larger mushrooms; leave small ones whole. About 5 minutes before the polenta is done, heat the olive oil in a frying pan and add the cracked garlic cloves. As the oil starts to smoke, add the mushrooms and immediately season them with salt and pepper. Cook, stirring occasionally, for 2–3 minutes, then add the chopped parsley and lemon juice. Discard the garlic. Tip the mushrooms out onto a plate, cover, and keep warm.

to finish   Once the polenta is cooked, fold in the butter and shredded cheese, then season with salt and pepper to taste.

to serve   Spoon the polenta into the center of four warmed plates and top with the mushroom fricassée. Sprinkle with extra shredded Gruyère.

as a main course   Prepare the soft polenta and mushroom fricassée as above. Season 8 quail. Heat a stovetop-to-oven casserole over a high heat until smoking. Add 2 tbsp oil and then the quail. Fry, turning with tongs, until lightly caramelized all over. Transfer to a preheated 450°F oven and roast for 5–6 minutes for medium-rare, or 8–10 minutes for well done. Remove from the oven and let rest for 10 minutes. Take the quail legs and breasts off the bone and serve piled on the polenta. Spoon the mushroom fricassée alongside.

as a canapé
Crush the dried Serrano ham into rough crumbs. Skewer the hot pan-roasted scallops on toothpicks, putting two or three on each stick. Quickly roll in the crisp ham crumbs and arrange on a plate drizzled with basil oil for dipping.

Scallops with basil oil & crisp serrano ham

SERVES 6

4 slices of Serrano ham

40 bay scallops

salt

1 tbsp olive oil

basil oil

1 cup basil leaves

½ cup olive oil

basil oil   Prepare this in advance. Blanch the basil leaves in boiling salted water for 25 seconds, then remove and drain well. Put into a blender with the olive oil and blend until smooth, 30–40 seconds. Pour the basil oil into a small jar and refrigerate. Bring to room temperature when ready to use.

Serrano ham   Preheat the oven to 375°F. Lay the ham slices in a single layer on a baking sheet lined with parchment paper. Cover with another sheet of parchment and place another baking sheet on top, to ensure the ham dries in flat sheets. Bake until crisp and dry, with little browning, 10–14 minutes. To check for doneness, break off a small piece and rub gently on a cool surface to see if it is crisp. Transfer the ham to a plate lined with paper towels and let cool.

pan-roasting the scallops   Pat the scallops dry on paper towels and season with salt. Heat a nonstick frying pan over a medium-high heat and add the 1 tbsp olive oil. When the oil is very hot but not smoking, add the scallops and cook for 25–30 seconds only. Gently move the delicate scallops in the pan with a wooden spoon as they cook, to sear evenly all over. Carefully transfer the cooked scallops to a plate lined with paper towels to drain.

to serve   Quickly streak the warmed plates with the basil oil and arrange the warm scallops on top. Break the crisp ham into pieces and scatter over the scallops. Serve immediately.

Oysters with shallot vinaigrette & watercress

SERVES 4

20 fresh oysters in shell

shallot vinaigrette

*2 large shallots, peeled and finely
diced*

*⅓ cup finest red wine vinegar
(preferably Cabernet Sauvignon)*

⅓ cup olive oil

salt

for serving

rock salt

handful of watercress leaves

shallot vinaigrette Make this a day in advance. In a small bowl, combine the shallots, wine vinegar, and olive oil. Add a pinch of salt, then cover and let infuse at room temperature overnight.

to shuck the oysters Hold an oyster in a folded cloth on a surface with the flatter shell up and the hinge pointing toward you. Force the tip of an oyster knife into the hinge of the shell, then carefully move it from side to side to work the shells apart—this takes some effort. Slide the blade of the knife along the inside of the upper shell until you come to the muscle, which attaches the oyster to the shell. Cut through this to detach the top shell. Holding the oyster over a bowl to catch any juices, lift off the top shell. Carefully run the blade of the knife under the oyster to loosen it, then clean away any broken fragments of shell.

to serve Whisk the vinaigrette to re-combine. Line each serving plate with a bed of rock salt and arrange five oysters on top. Spoon some of the reserved oyster juices and ½ tsp of the shallot vinaigrette over each oyster. Spoon the rest of the vinaigrette into four tiny serving dishes and place in the center of each plate (for guests to help themselves). Arrange the watercress leaves on top of the oysters and serve.

note Always buy a few extra oysters, as you cannot be sure that they will all be perfect. As you open each oyster, check that the flesh has a clean smell of the sea. If in any doubt, discard.

Mussels in a creamy sauce with basil

SERVES 4

2¼lb fresh mussels in shell

5 tbsp olive oil

*1 onion, peeled and roughly
    chopped*

*1 celery stalk, trimmed and roughly
    chopped*

*1 leek, white only, halved and
    roughly chopped*

4 garlic cloves, peeled and cracked

1¾ cups white wine

5 tbsp heavy cream

squeeze of lemon juice, to taste

salt and pepper

*large handful of basil leaves,
    chopped if desired*

to clean the mussels   Rinse the mussels under cold running water, scrubbing the shells thoroughly to remove sand and grit. Pull off the "beards" from the side of the shell. Tap any open mussels sharply with the back of a knife and discard those that do not close. Give the mussels a final rinse before cooking them.

to cook the mussels   Heat a large pot (one that will hold all the mussels and has a tight-fitting lid) and add 1 tbsp olive oil. Add the onion, celery, leek, and garlic. Stir, then cover and sweat over a low heat until soft, 8–10 minutes. Add the wine, increase the heat, and let bubble until reduced by two-thirds. Add the mussels, cover tightly, and steam until the shells have opened. Start checking after 3 minutes. Drain the mussels, reserving the cooking liquid, and discard any that remain closed. Tip the mussels into a large bowl; cover to prevent them from drying out.

for the sauce   Pour the cooking liquid into a small pan and bubble vigorously over a high heat until reduced by half. Add the cream, then pour into a blender. With the motor running, slowly add the remaining olive oil. When it is amalgamated, add a squeeze of lemon juice and season with salt and pepper to taste.

to serve   Add the cream sauce and basil to the mussels and toss to mix. Serve in large bowls, with plenty of fresh bread.

as a pasta dish   Peel, seed, and chop 4 ripe, flavorful tomatoes; set aside. Cook the mussels as above, then drain and remove from their shells while the cooking liquid is reducing. Meanwhile, cook 14oz linguine in plenty of boiling salted water until al dente. After blending the cream into the reduced liquid with the lemon juice and seasoning, return to the pan and add the shelled mussels and chopped tomatoes. Warm through very gently for a minute or two, if necessary, then divide among serving bowls. Drain the pasta, add to the bowls, and serve at once.

Mackerel with sweet & sour pepper jus

SERVES 4

4 mackerel fillets, about 4oz each

1 tbsp olive oil

salt and pepper

pepper jus

3 red bell peppers

1 yellow bell pepper

large pinch of sugar

1 tbsp heavy cream

juice of 1/2 lemon

1 1/2 tbsp unsalted butter, chilled and diced

1 tsp chopped marjoram or oregano

preparing the mackerel   Check over the mackerel fillets and remove any small bones with tweezers. Score the skin with a sharp knife in close parallel lines.

preparing the bell peppers   Using a swivel vegetable peeler, remove the skin from 1 red pepper and the yellow pepper. Halve these peppers and remove the core, seeds, and membrane, then cut the flesh into 1/4-inch dice and set aside. Halve, core, and seed the other peppers and remove the white membrane.

pepper jus   Purée the red pepper halves in a blender (or process in a juicer) and pass through a fine sieve. Put the pepper jus into a pan with the diced peppers, sugar, cream, a pinch of salt, and the lemon juice. Bring to a boil and bubble to reduce by two-thirds. Lower the heat and whisk in the cold butter, a piece at a time. Stir in the chopped marjoram, check the seasoning, and keep warm.

to cook the mackerel   Heat a large nonstick frying pan over a medium heat. Season the mackerel fillets with salt and pepper. Add the olive oil to the pan. When hot, place the seasoned mackerel fillets in the pan, skin-side down. Fry for 3 minutes, then turn the fillets over and continue frying until the mackerel is just cooked, about 1 minute more.

to serve   Place the mackerel fillets in the center of warmed plates and surround with the warm pepper jus. Serve at once.

as a main course   Bake a whole sea bass, about 2 1/4lb, to serve with the sweet and sour pepper jus. Season the cavity of the cleaned fish and stuff with 1/4 lime and 1/2 fennel bulb, chopped. Rub the skin with olive oil, season with salt and pepper, and wrap in foil. Place in a roasting pan and bake at 400°F until the flesh of the fish comes away easily from the bone, 25–30 minutes. Serve with the sweet and sour pepper jus.

Sardine frittata with green onions

SERVES 4

*8 fresh sardines, about 4oz each,
  scaled, gutted, and heads
  removed*
14oz all-purpose potatoes
1 tbsp unsalted butter
1 garlic clove, peeled and crushed
salt and pepper
*1/2 red onion, peeled and thinly
  sliced*
4 extra large eggs
1 tbsp all-purpose flour for dusting
2 tbsp olive oil
*2 green onions, trimmed and
  roughly chopped*
1/2 cup sour cream

preparing the sardines   Rinse the fish thoroughly and pat dry with paper towels. Lightly score the skin side with a small, sharp knife. Preheat the oven to 425°F.

to cook the potatoes   Peel and thinly slice the potatoes. Heat a 9 to 10-inch stovetop-to-oven casserole. When hot, add the butter followed by the garlic. When the butter is sizzling, add the potatoes and season with salt and pepper. Sauté, turning the potato slices frequently, until lightly browned on both sides, 3–4 minutes. Add the red onion and sauté for 2 minutes longer.

making the frittata   Break the eggs into a bowl, season with salt and pepper, and whisk lightly with a fork. Pour over the sautéed potato slices. Place in the oven to cook until the eggs are just set, 3–5 minutes.

pan-frying the sardines   Season the fish with salt and pepper, then dust with flour. Heat a nonstick frying pan and, when hot, add the olive oil. Lay the sardines in the pan and fry until golden brown and just cooked, about 1 minute on each side, depending on size.

to serve   Slide the frittata out of the pan onto a board and cut into four wedges. Place one wedge on each warmed plate and scatter the chopped green onions on top. Top with the pan-fried sardines and a generous spoonful of sour cream.

note   The frittata can be made in advance and served at room temperature, cut into small squares, as a canapé.

Roasted skate wing with crispy capers

SERVES 4

*2 skate wings, about 1lb each,
  trimmed and halved*

salt and pepper

4 tbsp olive oil

3–4 rosemary sprigs

1/2 cup capers, rinsed and drained

4 tbsp butter

juice of 1/2 lemon

3 tbsp chopped parsley

*4 tbsp aged balsamic vinegar
  (see note)*

to cook the skate   Preheat the oven to 425°F. Pat the skate portions dry with paper towels and season both sides with salt and pepper. Heat a large, wide, nonstick stovetop-to-oven casserole over a high heat. When hot, add 2 tbsp of the olive oil and the rosemary sprigs. Put the skate wings in the pan, thickest side down, and fry until golden brown, about 2 minutes. Turn the fish over and cook for 2 minutes longer. Transfer the pan to the oven to cook for 2 minutes.

to finish   Move the fish to a warmed plate to rest for a few minutes; discard the rosemary. Drain off the oil from the pan, then add 2 tbsp fresh olive oil and place over a high heat. When the oil is very hot, add the capers and fry until crisp, 30–45 seconds. Remove the capers with a slotted spoon and drain on paper towels. Add the butter to the pan and, when it starts to foam, stir in the lemon juice.

to serve   Arrange the skate on warmed plates. Scatter the crispy capers and chopped parsley on top and spoon the lemon butter sauce over. Drizzle the balsamic vinegar on the plates to finish.

note   If you do not have any aged balsamic, use twice the amount of standard balsamic vinegar and bubble over a medium-high heat to reduce by half, until syrupy.

as a main course   Simply double the quantities and serve with spinach or salicornia and creamy mash. Alternatively, make the recipe as above and serve each skate wing portion topped with a few slices of crisp belly pork (page 98); accompany with a portion of apple and frisée salad and creamy mash.

Seared salmon with cauliflower purée

Illustrated on page 56

SERVES 4

4 thick pieces of salmon fillet,
about 4oz each, skinned

salt and black pepper

2 tbsp olive oil

squeeze of lemon juice

cauliflower purée

1lb cauliflower, roughly chopped

2 cups milk

2/3 cup heavy cream

salt and white pepper

for garnish

chervil sprigs

preparing the salmon   Check over the salmon and remove any small bones with tweezers.

cauliflower purée   Put the chopped cauliflower, milk, and cream into a medium saucepan. Add a pinch of salt and bring to a simmer. Simmer gently until the cauliflower is very tender and the liquid has reduced by half, 10–12 minutes. Drain the cauliflower, reserving the liquid. Put the cauliflower into a blender with 2/3 cup of the cooking liquid and blend to a purée. If necessary, blend in a little more liquid to obtain a thick pourable consistency. Pass through a fine sieve into a bowl, pressing the cauliflower purée through with the back of a ladle or spoon. Season with salt and white pepper to taste and keep warm.

pan-frying the salmon   Season the fillets with salt and black pepper. Heat a nonstick frying pan over a high heat, and add the olive oil. When hot, add the salmon fillets and cook until lightly caramelized around the edges, 2–3 minutes on each side. Drain on paper towels and finish with a squeeze of lemon juice.

to serve   Flake the salmon and arrange on each warmed plate. Spoon a generous portion of cauliflower purée alongside. Garnish with chervil and grind a little black pepper over the salmon.

as main course fish cakes   *Illustrated on page 57*

Omit the cauliflower purée. Cook the salmon fillets as above; cool, then flake. Cook 14oz potatoes in boiling salted water until tender, then drain and dry over a low heat. Mash or rice into a bowl. Add the flaked salmon, 2 large egg yolks, juice of 1/2 lemon, 2 tbsp softened butter, 2 tbsp chopped chives, 2 tsp chopped capers (optional), and plenty of seasoning. Mix well, then shape into 8 patties and dust with flour. Dip into beaten egg, then into fresh white bread crumbs to coat. Heat 4 tbsp oil in a large frying pan and fry the fish cakes until crisp and golden, turning once. Drain on paper towels and serve with pickled cauliflower (page 10) and a watercress salad.

Poached cod with chive scrambled eggs

SERVES 4

7oz cod fillet, skinned

2 cups milk

1 tsp sea salt

1/2 onion, peeled

2 garlic cloves, peeled

1 bay leaf

1 thyme sprig

5 black peppercorns

scrambled eggs

6 eggs

salt and pepper

3 tbsp unsalted butter

4 tbsp heavy cream

1 tbsp chopped chives

for serving

*4 slices of white bread or brioche,
   freshly toasted*

poaching the cod   Check over the cod and remove any residual bones with tweezers. Put the milk, salt, onion, garlic, bay leaf, thyme, and peppercorns into a wide saucepan. Bring to a simmer, then remove from the heat and let infuse for 10 minutes. Add the cod to the infused liquid and simmer very gently (the surface of the liquid should barely move) until just cooked, 6–8 minutes. When ready, carefully remove the cod to a warmed plate and keep warm.

scrambling the eggs   Prepare these while the cod is poaching. Beat the eggs with a little salt and pepper. Melt the butter in a nonstick saucepan over a low heat. Pour in the eggs and stir constantly with a wooden spoon until almost scrambled. Stir in the cream and three-fourths of the chives, and remove from the heat. Check the seasoning and immediately remove the scrambled eggs from the pan to prevent further cooking.

to serve   Put a slice of hot toast on each warmed plate and pile the scrambled eggs on top. Divide the warm cod into chunky flakes and arrange on the eggs. Sprinkle with the rest of the chives.

note   As an alternative, use haddock fillet. For a more substantial fish course, double the quantities and serve with new potatoes tossed with melted butter and chopped dill.

as a main course
Omit the avocado. Pan-fry 4 chicken breast halves with the red onion until golden, 3–5 minutes. Transfer to a roasting pan and bake at 400°F for 20 minutes. Top with the mozzarella and almonds. Continue baking until the chicken is cooked through, about 5 more minutes. Meanwhile, cook the spinach in a covered pan until starting to wilt, about 30 seconds. Toss with the red onion and pile onto plates. Top with the sun-dried tomatoes, basil, bacon, and chicken.

Warm chicken, baby spinach & mozzarella salad

SERVES 4

2 skinless boneless chicken breast
*   halves*
salt and pepper
4 slices of bacon
½ cup sliced almonds
1 large ripe avocado
lemon juice for sprinkling
2 tbsp olive oil
½ red onion, peeled and finely
*   diced*
8oz baby spinach leaves, washed
8 boconccini mozzarella, halved,
*   or 1 large buffalo mozzarella,*
*   sliced*
6 basil leaves, sliced
12 sun-dried tomatoes, cut into
*   strips*
4 tbsp vinaigrette (page 157)

preparing the chicken Cut the chicken breasts crosswise into slices. Season the chicken with salt and pepper.

the bacon, almonds, and avocado Preheat the oven to 425°F. Lay the bacon slices side by side on a sturdy baking sheet. Place another heavy baking sheet on top to keep them flat and cook in the oven until crisp, 8–12 minutes; drain on paper towels. Scatter the almonds on a baking sheet and toast in the oven until lightly golden, 5–6 minutes. Halve, pit, and peel the avocado, then slice and toss in a little lemon juice to prevent discoloration; set aside.

sautéeing the chicken Heat a large nonstick frying pan or wok until smoking hot. Add the olive oil and then the chicken and sauté until lightly colored, 2–3 minutes. Add the red onion and continue cooking over a low heat until the chicken is cooked through and the onion is soft, 5–6 minutes, stirring frequently to ensure the onion doesn't burn.

assembling the salad Add the spinach to the pan, then immediately remove from the heat. Add the mozzarella, almonds, basil, and sun-dried tomatoes. Toss and stir until the spinach starts to wilt and the cheese begins to melt. Check the seasoning.

to serve Divide the warm salad among warmed plates and drizzle with the vinaigrette. Arrange the avocado slices and bacon on top, breaking the crisp bacon into smaller pieces, if desired. Serve immediately, with warm crusty bread.

Warm salad of arugula & lamb with garlic crisps

SERVES 4

14oz boneless loin of lamb,
*   trimmed*
salt and pepper
2 tbsp vegetable oil

garlic crisps
16 large garlic cloves
1¼ cups milk
vegetable oil for deep-frying

arugula salad
7oz small arugula leaves
1 tbsp olive oil
3 tsp balsamic vinegar

preparing the lamb   Preheat the oven to 400°F. Season the lamb with salt and pepper, and set aside.

garlic crisps   Cut the garlic cloves into wafer-thin slices and put into a small pan with half of the milk. Bring to a boil, then strain off the milk and discard. Add the rest of the milk and repeat the process. Drain the garlic in a fine strainer and rinse under cold running water to remove all milk residue. Drain and pat dry on paper towels. Heat the oil in a deep-fryer or other suitable deep pot to 300°F. When hot, fry the garlic slivers in two small batches until they just start to color, 5–6 minutes. Remove with a slotted spoon and drain on paper towels.

roasting the lamb fillet   Heat a wide stovetop-to-oven casserole until smoking hot, then add the 2 tbsp vegetable oil. Add the lamb and sear, turning, until lightly golden on all sides, about 2 minutes. Place the pan in the hot oven and roast the lamb for 2–3 minutes for medium rare, or 3–5 minutes for medium. Remove from the oven and let the meat rest for 10 minutes.

arugula salad   Put the arugula leaves in a bowl and dress with the olive oil and 1 tsp of the balsamic vinegar. Season with a pinch of salt and a twist of black pepper.

to serve   Thinly slice the lamb and arrange on serving plates. Scatter the arugula salad and garlic crisps over the meat and drizzle with the remaining balsamic vinegar. Serve at once.

as a main course Buy 2 Frenched racks of lamb, each with 6–8 chops. Heat 1 tbsp oil in a roasting pan in a 425°F oven. Add the racks, fat-side down, and roast for 15 minutes. Turn over and roast for 15–20 minutes longer. Let rest for 5 minutes. Drain off fat from the pan, then stir in a splash of red wine and 1 cup of stock to make a jus. Wilt the arugula in a covered pan for 20 seconds, then toss with the garlic crisps. Mound on plates, add the racks, and drizzle with the pan jus.

simple & satisfying

Chilled pumpkin & ginger soup

Wild mushroom & parsley broth

Celery root & parmesan soup

Braised lettuce with olive oil pomme purée

Seasonal vegetables in an herb nage

Herb-poached new potatoes with asparagus

Caramelized endive tart with walnut & roasted pear

Pan-fried gnocchi with tomato fondue & parmesan

Roasted shallot & baby beet salad

Lasagna of wild mushrooms with garlic purée

Jerusalem artichoke mousse with peas

Spaetzle topped with poached egg

Pumpkin & parmesan risotto with bay scallops

Squid with crushed potatoes & saffron vinaigrette

Tea-smoked salmon with herb mayonnaise

Smoked bacon risotto with corn & parmesan

Warm salad of duck breast & prunes with walnuts

Sautéed rabbit with arugula salad & carrot jus

Crisp pork belly with apple & frisée salad

Chilled pumpkin & ginger soup

SERVES 6

7 tbsp unsalted butter

*2lb peeled, seeded, and roughly
   chopped fresh pumpkin
   (about 7 cups)*

*3/4-oz piece fresh ginger, peeled
   and roughly sliced*

1/3 cup granulated sugar

salt and pepper

1/4 cup dry white wine

4 cups chicken stock (page 156)

5 tbsp heavy cream

crystallized ginger

1 1/2-oz piece fresh ginger, peeled

*2 tbsp confectioners' sugar, plus
   a little extra for dusting*

oil for deep-frying

pumpkin and ginger soup   Melt the butter in a heavy-based saucepan. Add the chopped pumpkin, ginger, sugar, and 1 tsp salt. Stir, then cover with a tight-fitting lid and sweat over a low heat for about 45 minutes, stirring occasionally. Remove the lid and continue cooking to reduce the liquid until the pumpkin is almost dry. Add the white wine and reduce by two-thirds, then add the chicken stock and cream, and cook for 10 minutes. Cool slightly, then purée the soup in a blender until smooth. Pass through a fine sieve into a bowl and let cool. Cover and chill.

crystallized ginger   Cut the ginger into julienne (or fine matchstick strips) and place in a bowl. Add the confectioners' sugar and toss to coat. Let stand for 45 minutes, turning from time to time. Tip the ginger into a strainer and rinse under cold running water to remove the sugar, then dry thoroughly on paper towels. Heat a 2-inch depth of oil in a small, deep, heavy pot to 300°F. Add the ginger julienne and deep-fry for 10 seconds, then remove immediately and drain on paper towels. Dust lightly with confectioners' sugar.

to serve   Check the seasoning, then ladle the soup into chilled bowls and garnish with the crystallized ginger.

note   This fresh-tasting soup is also delicious served hot. Simply warm through gently after puréeing and serve in warmed bowls, topped with the ginger garnish.

as a canapé Serve small portions of the soup—chilled or warm—in shot glasses. Halve the quantities for 8–10 canapé-sized portions. Omit the crystallized ginger garnish.

Wild mushroom & parsley broth

SERVES 4

2 tbsp unsalted butter

2 shallots, peeled and finely sliced

1/2 cup flat-leaf parsley leaves,
stems reserved

salt and pepper

4 cups chicken stock (page 156)

5oz mixed wild mushrooms, such
as chanterelles, porcini, and
shiitake, cleaned, trimmed, and
sliced if large

soft-poached eggs

1 tbsp vinegar

4 eggs

parsley broth   Put a wide, medium saucepan on a low heat and add 1 tbsp of the butter. When melted, add the shallots and reserved parsley stems (tied together), and season with salt and pepper. Stir, then cover and sweat gently for 20 minutes, stirring occasionally. Add the chicken stock and bring to a simmer, then skim and discard the parsley stems.

mushrooms   Heat a frying pan until very hot, then add the remaining butter and sauté the wild mushrooms until lightly colored all over, about 2 minutes. Add the mushrooms to the broth and let simmer gently for 10 minutes, skimming as necessary. Add the parsley leaves and simmer for 6–8 minutes longer. Check the seasoning.

soft-poached eggs   Cook these one at a time, while the broth is simmering. Two-thirds fill a deep pot with water, add the vinegar, and bring to a simmer. Stir the water to create a circular movement, then slide in an egg and cook until softly poached, 1 1/2–2 minutes. Carefully lift out and refresh in a bowl of ice water. Repeat with the rest of the eggs.

to serve   When the broth is ready, take it off the heat. Immediately add the soft-poached eggs, using a slotted spoon to transfer them, and warm through for 20 seconds. Ladle the soup into warmed bowls, placing a poached egg in the center of each one. Serve immediately.

as a canapé   This soup is a great way to appreciate the intense flavors of wild mushrooms and it can easily be down-sized to serve as an original canapé. Halve the quantities for 8 canapé-sized portions. Chop the parsley leaves and mushrooms, rather than leaving them whole. Serve the soup in coffee cups, each one topped with a soft-poached quail egg.

Celery root & parmesan soup

SERVES 6

8oz celery root, trimmed

5 tbsp unsalted butter

salt and pepper

*1 cup freshly grated Parmesan
   cheese, plus shavings for garnish*

3 cups chicken stock (page 156)

1 cup heavy cream

*2 tbsp truffle oil, plus extra
   for drizzling*

the soup base   Peel and roughly dice the celery root. Melt the butter in a medium pan over a low heat. Add the celery root with a pinch of salt and stir, then cover and sweat until soft, about 20 minutes, stirring occasionally. Add the grated Parmesan and chicken stock, and bring to a low simmer. Cook gently for 5 minutes.

to enrich and purée   Stir in the cream and truffle oil, and simmer for 5 minutes longer. Let cool slightly, then purée the soup in a blender until velvety smooth. Pass through a fine sieve into a clean pan or bowl.

to serve   Warm the soup gently, or let cool and chill if serving cold. Taste and adjust the seasoning. Top each portion with a drizzle of truffle oil and a few Parmesan shavings.

variation   Omit the grated Parmesan and truffle oil. Add 4oz smoked haddock (finnan haddie) fillet when the stock has come to a simmer. Continue as above, enriching with cream and puréeing the soup as described. Serve hot.

Braised lettuce with olive oil pomme purée

SERVES 4

braised lettuce

8 baby heads of romaine lettuce

4 tbsp unsalted butter

*8oz smoked Canadian bacon,
   roughly chopped (optional)*

*1 onion, peeled and roughly
   chopped*

*1 carrot, peeled and roughly
   chopped*

1 thyme sprig

*1¼ cups vegetable nage or chicken
   stock (page 156)*

pomme purée

1lb baking potatoes

salt and pepper

⅔ cup olive oil

4 tbsp unsalted butter

½ cup warm milk

braised lettuce   Preheat the oven to 400°F. Remove any loose outer leaves from the lettuce. Heat a large stovetop-to-oven casserole over a high heat, then add the butter. When it is sizzling and just turning brown, add the lettuce and turn to color on all sides; remove and set aside. Add the bacon to the pot, if using, and sauté until colored, 2–3 minutes. Add the onion, carrot, and thyme. Fry gently for about 5 minutes to soften, then return the lettuce to the pot. Pour in the nage or stock, cover with foil, and braise in the oven for 12–15 minutes. Remove from the oven and let stand for 10 minutes before serving.

pomme purée   Prepare this while the lettuce is braising. Peel the potatoes, cut into large, similar-sized pieces, and place in a saucepan. Cover with cold water, add salt, and bring to a boil. Lower the heat and simmer gently until tender, 15–20 minutes; drain. Rice the potato into a clean saucepan. Place over a low heat and slowly beat in the olive oil and butter, then stir in the warm milk. Check the seasoning.

to serve   Spoon the pomme purée onto warmed plates, arrange the lettuce on top, and drizzle with the cooking liquid.

as a tart   Follow the recipe for caramelized chicory tart (page 76), but using the braised lettuce in place of the chicory, roasted baby shallots instead of pears, and walnuts rather than pine nuts. Serve drizzled with the pan juices.

as a main course   Braised lettuce with olive oil pomme purée is an excellent accompaniment to roasted pork tenderloin. Season 2 tenderloins and quickly brown in a little oil in a frying pan over a high heat. Transfer to a roasting pan and roast in a preheated 400°F oven until tender and cooked through, 15–20 minutes. Remove from the oven and let rest for 5 minutes or so, then slice and serve with the braised lettuce and pomme purée.

Seasonal vegetables in an herb nage

SERVES 4–6

herb nage
3 onions
6 carrots
3 leeks, white part only
2 fennel bulbs
3 celery stalks
3 shallots
6 tarragon sprigs
6 parsley sprigs
1 tsp coriander seeds
12 black peppercorns
4 star anise

spring/summer vegetables
1 cup shelled fresh peas
1 cup shelled fresh fava beans
5oz sugar snap peas or
    snow peas
1 bunch of baby carrots (about 12),
    trimmed and scraped
12 baby turnips, trimmed
few small celery stalks or baby
    leeks, trimmed

to finish
7 tbsp butter, chilled and diced
salt
squeeze of lemon juice
chopped parsley or chervil, or
    celery leaves

herb nage   Peel and roughly chop all the vegetables, place in a large pot, and add enough cold water to cover. Add the herbs and spices. Cover the surface with a piece of parchment paper and bring to a boil over a medium heat. Reduce the heat and simmer gently for about 20 minutes. Remove from the heat and let cool, then cover with plastic wrap and refrigerate overnight.

the next day   Strain the nage through a fine sieve, discarding the vegetables and flavorings. Cover and keep in the fridge until ready to use.

blanching the vegetables   Bring a pan of salted water to a boil and cook the vegetables separately until al dente: 3–4 minutes for peas and fava beans; 2–3 minutes for sugar snaps or snow peas; 7–8 minutes for carrots and turnips; and about 10 minutes for celery stalks and baby leeks. Drain and immediately refresh each vegetable in ice water.

to serve   When ready to serve, pour 2 cups nage into a medium saucepan and bring to a boil. Whisk in the butter, a piece at a time, until emulsified. Season with salt and add lemon juice to taste. Add the blanched vegetables and warm through for 3–4 minutes. Serve in warmed bowls, finished with a sprinkling of chopped herbs or celery leaves.

as an autumn or winter starter   Choose vegetables at their seasonal best. The illustrated combination works well: 4oz rutabaga; 4–6 small parsnips; 4–6 small carrots; 4–6 medium new potatoes; and 4oz celery stalks. Peel the rutabaga, parsnips, and carrots; scrub the potatoes; and trim and halve the celery stalks. Cut the rutabaga in half, then slice. Leave small parsnips and carrots whole; halve larger ones. Cook all the vegetables separately in boiling salted water until al dente: 15–20 minutes for the rutabaga, parsnips, carrots, and potatoes, depending on size; and about 10 minutes for the celery. Drain and refresh in ice water, then warm through in the buttery nage for serving.

Herb-poached new potatoes with asparagus

SERVES 4

16–20 new potatoes, scrubbed
4 cups vegetable nage (page 156)
½ garlic bulb (cut horizontally)
salt
1 medium bunch of chervil
1 small bunch each of thyme,
  parsley, and tarragon
12 medium asparagus spears
4 tbsp unsalted butter, chilled and
  diced
shavings of Parmesan cheese for
  serving (optional)

herb-poached new potatoes   Put the potatoes into a large saucepan with the nage, garlic, and a pinch of salt; there must be enough liquid to cover the potatoes. Reserve half of the chervil and a little of each of the other herbs; tie the rest in a bundle with kitchen string and add to the pan. Bring to a gentle simmer, cover, and cook until the potatoes are tender, 12–15 minutes. Drain the potatoes and set aside, reserving 1 cup of the cooking liquid. Bring this to a boil in a small pan and reduce by half; strain back into the large pan and set aside.

the asparagus   While the potatoes are cooking, trim the woody ends from the asparagus, then peel the lower end of the stalks. Blanch in a small, deep pan of boiling water (so the stalks cook in the water, while the tips steam gently) until just tender, about 3 minutes. Drain and refresh in ice water, then drain on paper towels.

to serve   Chop the reserved thyme, parsley, and tarragon, and a little of the chervil. Whisk the butter into the reduced cooking liquid over a low heat. Add the potatoes, asparagus, and chopped herbs, and gently warm through. Arrange the potatoes on warmed plates and top with the asparagus. Garnish with chervil and drizzle the reduced cooking liquid over. Scatter the Parmesan shavings on top, if using, and serve immediately.

Caramelized endive tart with walnut & roasted pear

SERVES 4

7 tbsp unsalted butter

2 large heads Belgian endive,
halved lengthwise

salt and pepper

1 cup chicken stock (page 156)

1 cup walnut halves

4 ripe Comice or Bartlett pears

1 tbsp sugar

squeeze of lemon juice

9oz frozen puff pastry (about
½ package), thawed

caramelized endive   Place a large frying pan over a medium heat, then add 6 tbsp of the butter. Season both sides of the endive halves, then place cut-side down in the pan. Cook until golden brown, 6–7 minutes, then flip over and cook for 2 minutes longer. Drain off excess butter from the pan, then add the chicken stock and simmer until the endive is cooked and the liquid is reduced to a glaze, 6–7 minutes. Check the seasoning and let cool.

toasted walnuts   Preheat the oven to 400°F. Scatter the walnuts on a baking sheet and toast in the oven for 5–6 minutes. Season with salt and set aside to cool. When cool, roughly chop the nuts.

pan-roasted pears   Peel, core, and roughly chop or slice the pears. Place a large frying pan over a medium heat and add the remaining butter. When foaming, add the pears and cook, stirring occasionally, until evenly colored on all sides, 4–5 minutes. Tip out half of the butter, then return the pan to the heat. Add the sugar and stir for 30 seconds or so until it dissolves. Stir in 2 tbsp water to deglaze. Finish with a squeeze of lemon juice.

assembling the tarts   Roll out the puff pastry to a rectangle ¼-inch thick. Cut into 4 rectangles that are about ¾ inch larger all around than the cut endive. Place on a baking sheet and prick the pastry all over with a fork. Lay an endive half, cut-side up, in the centre of each pastry rectangle and press gently into the pastry; save any endive pan juices. Bake the tarts until the pastry is golden brown and risen around the edges, 15–17 minutes.

to serve   Place the tarts on warmed plates. Spoon the pan-roasted pear mixture on top and sprinkle with the chopped walnuts. Drizzle any reserved pan juices over and serve warm.

as a main course
Omit the pastry. Halve 2 squab chickens lengthwise, season, and pan-fry, skin-side down, in a little hot butter until deep golden, about 5 minutes. Turn and cook on the other side for 1–2 minutes, then roast in the oven at 400°F for about 15 minutes. Let rest for 10 minutes, then serve with the caramelized endive, roasted pears, walnuts, and pan juices. The flavor combination works brilliantly.

as a canapé Shape the gnocchi mixture into a slightly thinner roll. Once cooked, cut into 1-inch disks and pan-fry until golden brown, as described. Place on a tray and top each one with a little tomato fondue and a sliver of Parmesan. Serve warm, as an elegant canapé.

Pan-fried gnocchi with tomato fondue & parmesan

SERVES 4–6

gnocchi

3 large baking potatoes, about
*   1³/₄lb in total*
1 cup all-purpose flour, sifted
1 heaped cup freshly grated
*   Parmesan cheese*
1 whole egg, plus 2 egg yolks
3 tbsp minced chives
salt

tomato fondue

1 small bunch of thyme sprigs
1 small bunch of rosemary sprigs
4 tbsp olive oil
¹/₂ onion, peeled and finely diced
2 garlic cloves, peeled and cracked
salt and pepper
5 large plum tomatoes, peeled and
*   roughly chopped*

to assemble

¹/₄ cup all-purpose flour for
*   dusting*
4 tbsp unsalted butter
2oz Parmesan cheese, shaved
handful of arugula leaves, tossed
*   in a little vinaigrette (page 157)*

gnocchi   Preheat the oven to 400°F. Prick the potato skins, then bake until tender, about 1 hour. Let cool. Halve the potatoes and scoop out the flesh. Pass this through a potato ricer or a medium sieve into a bowl. Add the flour, Parmesan, egg, egg yolks, and chives. Mix thoroughly using an electric mixer and season with salt to taste. Lay a large sheet of plastic wrap on a work surface. Spoon a 6- to 8-inch length of the gnocchi mixture on the wrap, just off-center. Roll up tightly in the wrap, then twist and tie the ends to secure. Repeat with the rest of the gnocchi mixture. Bring a large pan of water to a boil and cook the gnocchi rolls for 10 minutes. Remove with a slotted spoon and refresh in ice water.

tomato fondue   Tie the herb sprigs together in cheesecloth or with string. Put a medium saucepan over a low heat and pour in the olive oil. Add the onion, garlic, herbs, and a pinch of salt. Cover and sweat until the onion is soft, about 10 minutes, then add the chopped tomatoes. Gently simmer for 20 minutes, stirring occasionally, until the tomato fondue is well reduced, thick, and pulpy. Check the seasoning and discard the garlic. Remove from the heat and set aside.

to assemble   Unwrap the cooked gnocchi, cut into ³/₄-inch lengths, and dust with the flour. Heat a nonstick frying pan over a medium heat. Add the butter and heat until melted and light brown, then add the gnocchi and cook, turning occasionally, until golden brown, 3–5 minutes. Meanwhile, warm the tomato fondue in the microwave, or in a small pan over low heat. Drain the gnocchi on paper towels and arrange on warmed plates. Spoon the tomato fondue alongside and top with Parmesan shavings and arugula leaves. Serve at once.

note   Prepared in this way, the gnocchi rolls can be made ahead and kept wrapped in the fridge for up to 3 days; they can also be frozen. If you prefer not to use plastic wrap, simply roll the gnocchi mixture into small balls in the palm of your hand and drop straight into the boiling water, then continue as above.

Roasted shallot & baby beet salad

SERVES 4

2 banana shallots (see note)
2 tbsp unsalted butter
10oz chanterelles or other wild
*   mushrooms, cleaned*
¼ cup white wine vinegar
¼ cup sweet white wine
2 tsp chopped parsley
salt and pepper
2 bunches of baby beets
*   (see note)*
1¼ cups vegetable stock
1 tsp sugar
½ onion, peeled and roughly
*   diced*
1 garlic clove, peeled
2 tbsp olive oil
4 small handfuls of salad leaves,
*   such as baby beet leaves, baby*
*   chard, and arugula*
1 tbsp aged balsamic vinegar

roasted shallots   Preheat the oven to 325°F. Prick the shallots all over with a toothpick, but don't peel them. Place on a baking sheet and roast until soft, 30–40 minutes, depending on size.

pickled chanterelles   Heat a medium frying pan and add 1 tbsp unsalted butter. When melted, add a third of the mushrooms and sauté until lightly colored. Add the wine vinegar and reduce until almost dry. Add the wine and reduce until the mushrooms are coated with a glaze. Add the chopped parsley and season to taste, then tip onto a plate to cool.

poached beets   Pick off any leaves from the beets that are suitable for the salad; wash and reserve. Trim the beet tops, leaving on a tuft of the leafy stems, then peel. Put the beets into a small saucepan with 1 cup of the vegetable stock, the sugar, a pinch of salt, and a few twists of black pepper. Bring to a simmer and cook until tender, about 20 minutes. Let cool in the reduced cooking juices.

wild mushroom purée   Heat a small saucepan and add the remaining butter. When melted, add the onion and garlic with a pinch of salt. Cover and sweat over a low heat until very soft, 15–20 minutes. Meanwhile, place a large frying pan on a high heat and add 1 tbsp olive oil. Add the remaining chanterelles, season with salt, and sauté until they are just turning golden, 3–4 minutes; remove and drain on paper towels. Tip the mushrooms onto the softened onion, along with the remaining vegetable stock, and simmer for 3 minutes. Discard the garlic and cool slightly, then purée in a blender until smooth. Transfer to a bowl, check seasoning, and set aside.

to serve   Halve the roasted shallots lengthwise. Warm through in the oven or microwave along with the mushroom purée, if necessary. Dress the salad leaves with the remaining olive oil, the balsamic vinegar, and seasoning. Place the shallot halves on warmed plates and top with the warm mushroom purée; pile the salad at one end. Arrange the baby beets and pickled chanterelles alongside and drizzle with some of the beet juices.

note   If banana shallots are not available, use 12 large, regular shallots instead. Similarly, if you cannot find baby beets, substitute 2 regular beets; peel and cut into large dice before poaching.

Lasagna of wild mushrooms with garlic purée

SERVES 4

shallot stock

2 tbsp unsalted butter

3 shallots, peeled and minced

2 garlic cloves, peeled

5 thyme sprigs

2 cups vegetable nage or chicken
     stock (page 156)

garlic purée

3 garlic bulbs, separated into cloves
     and peeled

1 cup heavy cream

salt and pepper

a little milk (if needed)

creamed mushrooms

10oz mixed wild mushrooms, such
     as chanterelles, cèpes, and
     shiitake, cleaned and trimmed

1 tbsp olive oil

4 tbsp unsalted butter, chilled and
     diced

2 garlic cloves, peeled and cracked

1 small bunch of chervil

1 tbsp chopped thyme

1 tbsp chopped parsley

lasagna noodles

5oz thin, fresh pasta sheets
     (page 157) or 8 wonton wrappers

shallot stock　　Heat 1 tbsp butter in a pan over a low heat, and add the shallots, garlic, and thyme. Cover and sweat gently until soft, but not colored, 5–7 minutes. Add the nage or stock and simmer for 15 minutes. Remove from the heat and let infuse for 15 minutes. Discard the garlic and thyme; measure 1 cup stock. (Any remaining shallot stock can be frozen.)

garlic purée　　Put the garlic into a small pan, cover with cold water, and bring to a boil. Drain, and repeat this process three times. Return the garlic to the pan, add the cream with a pinch of salt, and bring to a low simmer. Cook gently, stirring occasionally, until the garlic is soft and the cream is reduced, about 15 minutes. Tip into a blender and purée until smooth, then pass through a fine sieve into a bowl. Check the seasoning and keep warm.

creamed mushrooms　　Quarter or slice any larger mushrooms. Heat the olive oil in a large frying pan over a high heat. Add 1½ tbsp of the butter and, once it starts foaming, add the garlic and mushrooms. Season with salt and pepper. Sauté until the mushrooms are tender, 3–4 minutes, then add the shallot stock and reduce by two-thirds. Meanwhile, set aside a few chervil sprigs for garnish; chop the rest of the leaves, discarding the stems. Remove the garlic from the mushrooms. Stir in the remaining butter to emulsify, add the chopped herbs, check the seasoning, and keep warm.

to serve　　Reheat the garlic purée gently in a small pan; it should have a pourable consistency, so thin with a little milk if it is too thick. If using pasta, cut into eight 4-inch squares. Add the pasta or wonton wrappers to a pan of boiling salted water and cook until al dente, 1–1½ minutes; drain well. Layer the lasagna on warmed plates, starting with a layer of creamed mushrooms, then a dab of garlic purée, then a square of pasta or a wonton wrapper. Repeat these layers and finish with a layer of mushrooms. Garnish with chervil sprigs and serve.

as a main course　　Lightly poach 2 skinless boneless chicken breast halves in chicken stock until tender, 15–20 minutes; let rest for a few minutes. Cook 4oz spinach leaves in a covered pan with 1 tbsp water until just wilted, 30–60 seconds; drain well, then chop. Slice the chicken and add to the creamed mushrooms along with the chopped spinach. Layer the lasagna as above.

Jerusalem artichoke mousse with peas

SERVES 6

1½lb Jerusalem artichokes
salt and pepper
juice of ½ lemon
1 whole egg, plus 2 egg yolks
⅔ cup heavy cream

to assemble
2 tsp softened butter
1 cup shelled fresh peas
Jerusalem artichoke crisps
  (page 13) for garnish (optional)

Jerusalem artichoke purée   Peel the artichokes and immediately place in a pan of cold salted water, with the lemon juice added to prevent discoloration. Bring to a boil, then lower the heat and simmer until the artichokes are tender, 15–20 minutes. Drain, then purée the artichokes in a blender. Transfer to a medium saucepan and bring to a simmer. Cook over a low heat until the artichoke purée is reduced by half and thickened. Set aside to cool. When cool, beat in the egg, egg yolks, and cream. Season with salt and pepper to taste.

baking the soufflés   Preheat the oven to 325°F. Grease 6 individual 1-cup soufflé dishes generously with softened butter. Spoon the artichoke mousse into the dishes to fill them by two-thirds. Set in a shallow roasting pan and surround with warm water to come halfway up the sides of the dishes. Bake until the mousses are lightly firm to the touch, 30–40 minutes.

cooking the peas   About 10 minutes before the mousses will be ready, add the peas to a pan of boiling salted water. Simmer until just tender, about 3 minutes; drain.

to serve   Place the soufflé dishes on warmed plates and spoon the peas on top of the mousses. Serve artichoke crisps as an extra garnish, if desired.

as a main course   Season a 3-lb roaster chicken with salt and pepper. Poach whole in a well-seasoned nage or chicken stock with a handful of tarragon sprigs until tender and cooked through, 40–50 minutes. Line the base of the soufflé dishes with parchment paper before greasing. Once cooked, run a knife around the mousses and unmold onto warmed large plates. Carve the chicken and serve with the mousses.

Spaetzle topped with poached egg

spaetzle

5 tbsp unsalted butter

1³/4 cups all-purpose flour

1 tsp salt

¹/2 tsp freshly grated nutmeg

2 whole eggs, plus 3 egg yolks

²/3 cup milk

dash of vegetable oil

soft-poached eggs

dash of vinegar

4 eggs

to finish

5 tbsp unsalted butter

¹/4 cup hazelnut oil

salt and pepper

the spaetzle mixture   Melt the butter in a small saucepan over a medium heat and cook until light golden brown. Remove from the heat. Combine the flour, salt, and nutmeg in a large bowl and make a well in the middle. In a separate bowl, whisk the eggs and egg yolks with the warm butter and milk, then slowly pour into the flour well. Gradually draw in the flour from the sides of the well with your fingers and mix to a soft dough. Cover and let rest in the fridge for 30 minutes.

to cook the spaetzle   Bring a large pan of salted water to a boil. Spread the dough on a chopping board or flat tray to an even ¹/8-inch thickness. You will need to cook the spaetzle in several batches. Hold the edge of the board or tray partly over the pan of boiling water. Using a metal spatula held at a 20° angle, cut off thin strips of dough and knock them into the water, about 15 or 20 at a time. (Alternatively, push the dough through a slotted spaetzle plate or colander directly into the water.) Cook for about 1 minute. Using a slotted spoon, lift out the cooked noodles and put into a bowl of ice water to cool; remove and drain. Place on a tray lined with paper towels to dry. Continue cooking in batches until the dough is used up. When finished, toss the noodles in a little oil to prevent them from sticking together. Reserve in the fridge.

soft-poached eggs   Half-fill a large, shallow pan with water, add the vinegar, and bring to a simmer. Stir the simmering water to create a circular movement, then poach the eggs until softly set, 1¹/2–2 minutes. Carefully remove and drain on paper towels; keep warm in a low oven.

to finish   While the eggs are poaching, place a sauté pan over a medium heat, add the butter, and cook until lightly browned. Immediately add the spaetzle and sauté for 2 minutes. Drizzle the hazelnut oil over and check the seasoning. Divide among warmed plates. Top with the poached eggs and flick a pinch of salt on top of each egg, then serve.

Pumpkin & parmesan risotto with bay scallops

SERVES 6

pumpkin stock

3 tbsp unsalted butter

2½ cups peeled, seeded, and
    roughly chopped pumpkin

½ cup roughly chopped
    Parmesan cheese

½ cup medium dry white wine

3 cups vegetable nage (page 156)

2 tbsp heavy cream

risotto

3 tbsp unsalted butter

½ onion, peeled and finely diced

1¼ cups arborio or other
    risotto rice

salt and pepper

8oz bay scallops

2 tbsp olive oil

squeeze of lemon juice

2 tbsp minced chives

3 tbsp freshly grated Parmesan
    cheese, plus shavings for garnish

pumpkin and Parmesan stock   Melt the butter in a large saucepan. Add the pumpkin and chopped Parmesan, cover, and sweat over a low heat, stirring occasionally until soft and watery, about 30 minutes. Remove the lid and simmer until the water has evaporated, then add the white wine and reduce by two-thirds. Add the stock and cream and simmer for 8–10 minutes. Cool slightly, then purée in a blender until smooth. Return to the pan and bring to a simmer.

the risotto   Heat half of the butter in a medium, nonstick saucepan. Add the onion, cover, and sweat until soft, 7–8 minutes. Add the rice and stir over the heat until the grains are translucent, about 2 minutes. Add the pumpkin stock, a small ladleful at a time, stirring constantly and waiting for each addition to be absorbed before adding the next. This process should take 15–20 minutes; the risotto is ready when the rice is al dente and the texture is creamy (you may not need all of the stock). Check the seasoning and finish with the remaining butter.

sautéeing the scallops   Pat the scallops dry with paper towels, then season lightly with salt. Heat a large frying pan over a high heat, then add the olive oil. Sauté the scallops in the hot oil until they just start to color at the edges, 30–45 seconds, then remove and drain on paper towels. Squeeze a little lemon juice over them.

to serve   Stir the chopped chives and grated Parmesan through the risotto. Spoon into warmed bowls and top with the sautéed scallops. Scatter Parmesan shavings over the scallops and serve immediately.

as a main course Increase the variety and quantity of shellfish. Try a mixture of scallops, shrimp, and cracked crab claws. Or cook 1lb each fresh mussels and small hardshell clams in a tightly covered pan with $^2/_3$ cup dry white wine and $^1/_2$ finely sliced shallot until the shells open, 3–4 minutes; discard any that remain closed. Drain and serve on top of the risotto.

Squid with crushed potatoes & saffron vinaigrette

SERVES 4

16–24 baby squid (4–6 per person),
depending on size (see note),
cleaned
14oz new potatoes
salt and pepper
4 tbsp unsalted butter
1 tbsp chopped parsley
1 tbsp chopped chives or dill
2 tbsp olive oil
juice of ¹/₂ lemon, or to taste

saffron vinaigrette
5 tsp white wine vinegar
large pinch of saffron threads
4 tbsp olive oil

saffron vinaigrette   Start this first. Put the wine vinegar into a small saucepan with 1 tsp water and the saffron threads. Bring to a boil over a medium heat, then immediately remove from the heat and set aside to infuse for 2 hours.

preparing the squid   Rinse the whole baby squid pouches and separate tentacles. Pat dry with paper towels and set aside.

crushed potatoes   Put the potatoes into a pan, cover with cold water, add salt, and bring to a boil. Lower the heat and simmer until just tender, 12–15 minutes. Drain the potatoes and peel while still warm, using a small knife. Return to the pan and crush the potatoes lightly with a fork. Add the butter and chopped herbs, and fork through. Season with salt and pepper to taste; keep warm.

sautéeing the squid   Heat a large, nonstick frying pan over a high heat, then add the 2 tbsp olive oil. When it is hot and almost on the point of smoking, add the squid and season with salt. Sauté until the squid are lightly colored and just cooked through, 1–1¹/₂ minutes. Add a generous squeeze of lemon juice and remove from the heat.

to serve   To finish the vinaigrette, stir in the 4 tbsp olive oil and a pinch of salt. Put a small mound of crushed potatoes in the center of each warmed serving plate. Arrange the squid on top and dress with the saffron vinaigrette. Serve immediately.

note   If baby squid are unavailable, use cleaned, full-sized squid; you will need 1lb prepared weight. Slice the body pouches into rings and cut the tentacles into smaller pieces, if necessary.

as a main course   Serve each portion with a pan-fried fillet of red mullet, sea bass, or porgy—the flavors complement each other perfectly. Buy 4 fish fillets, each about 4oz. Before you cook the squid, pan-fry the fish fillets, skin-side down, in a little hot butter and oil for 1¹/₂–2 minutes, then flip over and cook for 30 seconds or so longer. Let rest in a warm place while you cook the squid.

Tea-smoked salmon with herb mayonnaise

Illustrated on page 90

SERVES 4

tea-smoked salmon
1lb salmon fillet, trimmed and
  skinned
4 tbsp olive oil
salt and pepper
½ cup Lapsang Souchong tea
  leaves

herb mayonnaise
3 egg yolks
juice of ½ lemon
1 cup olive oil
1¼ cups grapeseed oil
10 tbsp chopped soft-leafed herbs,
  such as parsley, basil, tarragon,
  chervil, and dill

for serving
5oz baby salad leaves, such as
  spinach, chard, or arugula
dash of extra virgin olive oil
a little red wine vinegar
8 small, thin rounds of rye or
  multigrain bread, lightly toasted

herb mayonnaise   Prepare this in advance. Put the egg yolks, lemon juice, and 1 tsp salt into a bowl and beat together until smooth. Combine the olive and grapeseed oils. Slowly add the oils to the yolk mixture, drop by drop to begin with, then in a steady drizzle, beating constantly with a hand-held electric mixer to create an emulsion. (If the mixture splits, add 1 tsp boiling water to one side of the bowl and beat to re-emulsify.) Taste and adjust the seasoning. Finally, fold in the chopped herbs. This herb mayonnaise can be kept for up to 3 days in the fridge.

tea-smoked salmon   Use a large, deep pan (not your best one) or a wok with a tight-fitting lid. Check the salmon for pin bones and remove any with tweezers. Take a large sheet of foil and fold into 3 or 4 layers until it is just bigger than the salmon. Pierce the foil several times with a thin skewer and rub with a little oil. Season both sides of the salmon with salt and pepper, then lay it on the foil. Put the dry pan or wok over a high heat. When it is very hot, add the tea and stir with a spoon for 5–10 seconds to toast. Lay the foil holding the fish directly on top of the tea. Cover tightly with the lid and smoke the fish for at least 5 minutes, or up to 8 minutes for thick fillets. Lift out the salmon on the foil and brush with a little olive oil, then wrap in the foil and let rest for 5 minutes or so.

to serve   Dress the salad leaves with a dash of olive oil, a little red wine vinegar, and salt to taste. Flake the warm salmon. Place 2 toast rounds on each warmed serving plate. Top each with a generous spoonful of herb mayonnaise and then the salmon flakes. Finish with the salad leaves.

tea-smoked haddock as a main course   *Illustrated on page 91*

Hot-smoke 4 pieces of skinned haddock fillet, about 6oz each, as above, allowing an extra 3 minutes. Serve topped with a soft-poached egg (see page 85) and accompanied by the salad and herb mayonnaise. Or, simply hot-smoke 4 larger pieces of salmon fillet, about 6oz each, and serve with the herb mayonnaise and salad, or with asparagus tagliatelle (page 129).

Smoked bacon risotto with corn & parmesan

SERVES 4

bacon stock
1 tbsp unsalted butter
*1 large onion, peeled and roughly
    chopped*
2 garlic cloves, peeled
3 thyme sprigs
3 bay leaves
*12oz slab bacon, rind removed and
    roughly chopped*
4 cups chicken stock (page 156)

corn
1 ear of corn, shucked

risotto
1/2 cup diced bacon
4 tbsp unsalted butter
1/2 medium onion, finely diced
*scant 1 cup arborio or other
    risotto rice*
2 tbsp heavy cream
salt and pepper
*3/4 cup freshly grated Parmesan
    cheese for serving*

bacon stock   Melt the butter in a medium saucepan. Add the onion, garlic, thyme, and bay leaves. Stir, then cover and sweat over a low heat until the onion softens, about 10 minutes. Meanwhile, in a large frying pan, sauté the chopped bacon until golden brown. Drain on paper towels. Add the bacon to the onion, pour in the stock, and bring to a simmer. Continue to simmer for 20 minutes, skimming off any fat that rises to the surface. Strain the stock into a clean pan. Check the seasoning: If the stock tastes too salty, dilute it with a little water.

corn   While the stock is simmering, cook the corn in boiling water until the kernels are tender, about 10 minutes; don't add salt as it will toughen the corn. Drain. When cool enough to handle, hold the cob upright and shave off the kernels carefully, using a sharp knife. Keep warm.

risotto   In a frying pan, sauté the diced bacon over a medium heat until lightly colored. Drain on paper towels and set aside. Heat 3 tbsp butter in a medium, nonstick saucepan. Add the diced onion, cover, and sweat over a low heat until soft, 8–10 minutes. In the meantime, bring the bacon stock back to a simmer. Add the rice and sautéed bacon to the onion and stir over the heat for 2 minutes. Then start to add the stock in small ladlefuls, waiting for each addition to be absorbed before adding the next and stirring constantly. Continue adding the stock in this way until the risotto is creamy and the rice is al dente; it will take 15–20 minutes (you may not need all of the stock). Finish with the cream and remaining 1 tbsp butter. Check the seasoning.

to serve   Spoon the risotto onto warmed plates, scatter the corn kernels on top, and finish with grated Parmesan.

Warm salad of duck breast & prunes with walnuts

SERVES 4

½ cup walnut halves

salt and pepper

2 boneless duck breast halves,
with skin, about 6oz each

1 tbsp vegetable oil

2 tbsp unsalted butter

tea-infused prunes

2 English breakfast tea bags

finely pared zest and juice of
1 orange

2 cinnamon sticks

1 tbsp sugar

16 semi-dried Agen prunes

spinach salad

1½ cups baby spinach leaves

1 tbsp olive oil

squeeze of lemon juice

tea-infused prunes   Prepare these in advance. Put the tea bags and 2 cups water into a pan with the orange zest, orange juice, cinnamon sticks, and sugar. Slowly bring to a boil, then add the prunes and simmer for 5 minutes. Remove from the heat and let the prunes cool in the liquid. Let steep for at least 2 hours, but preferably overnight.

walnuts   Preheat the oven to 400°F. Scatter the walnuts on a baking sheet and toast in the oven for 6 minutes. Season the hot nuts with salt, then let cool. Break the nuts into smaller pieces.

pan-frying the duck breasts   Using a sharp knife, score the skin side of the duck breasts on the diagonal and again across this to make a diamond pattern on the skin. Season both sides of the duck breasts generously with salt and pepper. Place a nonstick frying pan over a medium heat and add the vegetable oil. Put the duck breasts in the pan, skin-side down, and cook until golden, about 5 minutes. Flip over and add 1 tbsp butter to the pan. Cook for 4–5 minutes longer for medium rare; 6–7 minutes for medium; or 10 minutes for well done. Remove the duck breasts from the pan and let rest in a warm place for 10 minutes.

spinach salad   Shred the spinach leaves and dress with a dash of olive oil and a squeeze of lemon juice. Season with salt and pepper.

to serve   Drain the prunes, reserving 5–6 tbsp of the liquid; discard the cinnamon and orange zest. Put the prunes and reserved liquid into a small saucepan and heat gently for a few minutes. Lift out the prunes and keep warm. Bring the liquid back to a boil, then reduce the heat and whisk in the remaining 1 tbsp butter to create an emulsion. Slice the duck breasts across the grain into thin slices. Arrange on warmed plates with the prunes and dressed spinach. Drizzle the duck with the tea-butter emulsion and scatter the toasted walnuts over the salad.

as a main course Pan-fry 4 duck breasts rather than 2, and make a rutabaga and potato gratin (page 108) to serve as an accompaniment. Cook the spinach leaves in a covered pan with a dash of water until just wilted, then drain. Place the duck breasts on warm plates with the wilted spinach, tea-infused prunes, and a portion of gratin. Top with the whole toasted walnuts, then serve.

Sautéed rabbit with arugula salad & carrot jus

SERVES 4

2 saddles of rabbit, about 14oz
each, boned and trimmed
(see note)
salt and pepper
1 tbsp unsalted butter

carrot jus

1¼ cups fresh carrot juice
(see note)
juice of ½ lemon
pinch of sugar
1 tbsp heavy cream
1 tbsp unsalted butter, chilled and
diced
2 tbsp tarragon leaves, finely
chopped

arugula salad

5oz arugula leaves, trimmed
1 tbsp olive oil
1 tbsp balsamic vinegar

carrot jus   Prepare this first. Pour the carrot juice into a small saucepan and add the lemon juice, sugar, cream, and a pinch of salt. Bring to a boil, then simmer to reduce by two-thirds. Whisk in the cold butter to emulsify. Taste and adjust the seasoning; keep warm.

sautéeing the rabbit   Season the rabbit tenderloins with salt. Heat a heavy-based frying pan over a medium heat, then add the butter. When melted and sizzling, add the rabbit tenderloins and sauté them until golden and cooked through, 5–6 minutes. Transfer to a warm plate, cover loosely with foil, and set aside to rest for 5–6 minutes.

arugula salad   Dress the arugula leaves with the olive oil and balsamic vinegar, seasoning with salt and pepper to taste.

to serve   Bring the carrot jus back to a simmer. Slice each rabbit tenderloin lengthwise into 3 slices. Arrange them in the center of warmed plates with the dressed arugula. Stir the tarragon into the carrot jus and spoon around the rabbit slices. Serve immediately.

note   Ask your butcher to bone the rabbit saddles; you should end up with 4 neat tenderloins. If you have an electric juicer, make your own carrot juice and strain it through a fine sieve. Or, buy fresh carrot juice.

as a main course   Ask your butcher to bone the hind legs of the 2 rabbits. Lay each flat on a buttered piece of foil. Season and sprinkle with a little chopped tarragon. Roll into a sausage shape, wrap in the foil, and roast at 425°F for about 15 minutes. Check that the rabbit is cooked through by inserting a small knife into the thickest part. Let rest for 5 minutes or so, then serve with the sautéed rabbit tenderloins, salad, and carrot jus.

Crisp pork belly with apple & frisée salad

SERVES 6

1³/₄lb fresh pork belly (ideally in one
    piece)

4 cups chicken stock (page 156)

¹/₂oz thyme sprigs

salt

mirepoix

2 bay leaves

3 garlic cloves, peeled

1 carrot, peeled and roughly
    chopped

1 onion, peeled and roughly
    chopped

1 celery stalk, roughly chopped

apple and frisée salad

7oz frisée (pale leaves only)

1 Granny Smith apple

1 tbsp olive oil

1 tbsp aged balsamic vinegar

salt and pepper

to finish

4 tsp unsalted butter

few rosemary sprigs

2 tbsp aged balsamic vinegar

preparing the pork   Soak the pork belly overnight in plenty of cold water. The next day, drain the pork and put into a cooking pot that is large enough to accommodate it with cooking liquid. Add 4 cups cold water and rapidly bring to a boil to blanch the pork. Pour off the water, then add the chicken stock, thyme, and 1 tsp salt. Add the mirepoix ingredients and bring to a low simmer. Skim, then cook at a low simmer for 3 hours, skimming the surface from time to time. If necessary, replenish the cooking liquid with water during cooking to ensure the pork stays covered. Remove from the heat and let the pork belly cool in the cooking liquid.

pressing the pork   When cool, take the pork belly out of the pot. Remove the skin and any bones, then lay the pork belly flat on a tray, or in a casserole large enough to take it flat. Cover the pork with another tray, or a container that fits inside the casserole, and press as hard as possible. Uncover, then wrap the pork tightly in plastic wrap and press between the trays (or containers) as before. Place in the fridge, weigh down with heavy objects, and leave overnight.

apple and frisée salad   Prepare this just before serving. Tear the pale frisée leaves into small pieces. Peel, core, and slice the apple into julienne and place in a bowl with the frisée. Drizzle the olive oil and balsamic vinegar over and toss to mix. Season with salt and pepper to taste.

to assemble   Unwrap the pork belly and cut into ³/₄-inch-thick slices, using a sharp knife. Season with salt. Heat the butter in a nonstick frying pan over a medium heat. Fry the pork belly in batches, with a few sprigs of rosemary, until golden and crisp. Drain the pork on paper towels, then arrange on plates with the salad. Add the balsamic vinegar to the pan juices and stir to deglaze, then drizzle over the salad and around the plate.

as a main course   This dish works exceptionally well as a winter main course—real comfort food. Simply double the quantities. Cut the pressed pork into large wedges, pan-fry, and serve with the apple salad and rich, buttery mashed potato.

as a canapé   Cut the pork into bite-sized chunks and pan-fry as above until crisp, then skewer onto wooden toothpicks and serve on a bed of apple and frisée salad.

food for groups

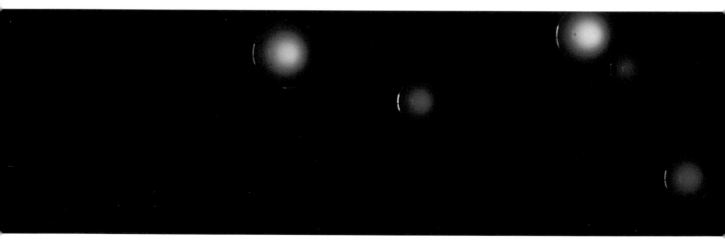

Ragout of cranberry beans & baby onions

Gazpacho consommé with scallop ravioli

Caramelized onion and mushroom tarts

Rutabaga & potato gratin with pine nuts

Terrine of herb-cooked leeks & crab salad

Anchovy & tomato terrine with basil purée

Blinis topped with curried oysters

Creamed salt cod & celery root soup

Crab croquettes with tomato dipping sauce

Home-cured salmon with grainy mustard dressing

Honey-glazed ham with celery root rémoulade

Oxtail & lentil ragout with root vegetables

Beef bourguignonne tartlets

Roasted lamb cannelloni with minted peas

Ragout of cranberry beans & baby onions

SERVES 6

*1 cup dried cranberry (borlotti) or
    navy beans, or a mixture,
    soaked in cold water overnight*

1 onion, peeled and quartered

1 carrot, peeled and quartered

*1 celery stalk, trimmed and
    quartered*

3 garlic cloves, peeled

5–6 thyme sprigs

*4-oz piece slab bacon, cut into
    large pieces*

8 cups chicken stock (page 156)

20 baby onions

*5 tbsp chilled unsalted butter, in
    pieces*

salt and pepper

lemon juice, to taste

*5–6 tarragon sprigs, leaves
    stripped and chopped*

to cook the beans   Drain the soaked beans, put them into a large pot, and cover with fresh cold water. Bring to a boil, then drain and return the beans to the pan. Add the onion, carrot, celery, garlic, thyme, and bacon. Pour in the stock, bring to a gentle boil, and cook, stirring occasionally, until the beans are tender, 1½–2 hours or longer. Remove from the heat and let the beans cool in the liquid for about 15 minutes. Strain the liquid into a large pan and reserve; set the beans aside.

to cook the baby onions   Immerse the onions in hot water for 30 seconds to loosen the skins, then peel. Return the reserved bean cooking liquid to the heat, add the baby onions, and simmer until tender, 10–12 minutes. Remove the onions with a slotted spoon and set aside.

to finish   Bring the liquid back to a boil and boil to reduce by half. In the meantime, remove the bacon, vegetables, garlic, and thyme from the beans and discard. Whisk the cold butter into the reduced cooking liquid, a piece at a time, to emulsify the sauce. Add the beans and baby onions, and simmer for a few minutes to warm through—the ragout should have a thick, souplike consistency.

to serve   Season with salt and pepper, and add a squeeze of lemon juice to taste. Stir in the chopped tarragon and serve in warmed bowls, with crusty bread, if desired.

as a main course   Increase all the ingredient quantities by half. Serve each portion of ragout topped with a seared thick slice of fois gras, or a pan-fried small cod fillet, or 1 or 2 fried good-quality, fresh pork sausages.

Gazpacho consommé with scallop ravioli

SERVES 4

2¼lb vine-ripened tomatoes, roughly chopped

1 small red onion, peeled and roughly diced

½ hot red chili pepper, seeded and chopped

1 small garlic clove, peeled and crushed

1 red bell pepper, cored, seeded, and roughly chopped

1 English cucumber

¼ cup red wine vinegar

½ cup tomato juice

7 tbsp olive oil

⅔ cup cilantro leaves

1½ tbsp sugar

salt

scallop ravioli (optional)

1 quantity fresh pasta dough (page 157), or 10-oz package wonton wrappers

12 bay scallops

1 egg, beaten

for serving

1 tomato, peeled, seeded, and finely diced

4 tbsp olive oil

about 20 small basil leaves

gazpacho base   Put the tomatoes into a large bowl with the onion, chili, garlic, and bell pepper. Peel the cucumber, halve lengthwise, and scoop out the seeds. Roughly chop the cucumber flesh and add to the tomatoes. Add the wine vinegar, tomato juice, olive oil, cilantro, sugar, and salt to taste. Using an immersion blender, slowly break up the ingredients. Increase the speed and blend for about 3 minutes to make a smooth, thick soup. Cover and refrigerate overnight to let the flavors develop.

to clarify   The next morning, pour the soup into a cheesecloth-lined strainer set over a large, clean bowl. Put this into the fridge and leave undisturbed to let the liquid slowly drip through the cheesecloth. This will take about 3 hours; don't be tempted to squeeze the cloth to hasten the process or the consommé will be cloudy. Once it has dripped through, discard the residue.

scallop ravioli   Bring a large pan of salted water to a boil, and have a bowl of ice water ready. Meanwhile, roll out the pasta, if using, until very thin. Cut out 24 small disks, 1¾ inches in diameter, from the pasta or wonton wrappers. Place a scallop in the center of half of the disks. Brush the pasta or wonton edges lightly with beaten egg. Top with the remaining disks and gently press out the air bubbles and to seal the edges. Blanch the ravioli in the boiling water for 45 seconds, then remove and refresh in the ice water. Drain on paper towels, then cover and refrigerate until needed.

to serve   Pour the consommé into a saucepan and heat gently until just hot, but not simmering. Slip in the scallop ravioli and gently warm through in the soup for about 1 minute. Ladle the soup into warmed bowls, placing 3 ravioli in each bowl. Add the diced tomato and drizzle 1 tbsp olive oil over each serving. Scatter the basil leaves on top.

to serve as a classic gazpacho   Skip the clarifying and you have a flavorful classic gazpacho with a good, thick texture, which can easily be upsized to serve larger gatherings. Omit the ravioli and stir the soup well after refrigerating overnight. Pour into bowls and add a drizzle of basil oil (page 47). Accompany with small bowls of croûtons and diced sweet onions and red bell peppers, for guests to help themselves.

Caramelized onion and mushroom tarts

SERVES 4

shallot stock
4 tsp unsalted butter
3 shallots, peeled and minced
2 garlic cloves, peeled
5 thyme sprigs
2 cups vegetable nage or chicken stock (page 156)

caramelized onions
4 tbsp unsalted butter
1 garlic clove, peeled
2 onions, peeled and thinly sliced
salt and pepper

tart bases
8oz frozen puff pastry (about ½ package), thawed
2 tsp thyme leaves (optional)
1 egg, beaten with 1 tsp water

mushroom topping
14oz mixed mushrooms, such as crimini, chanterelle, shiitake, and oyster, cleaned
5 tbsp unsalted butter, chilled
2 garlic cloves, peeled
1 tbsp heavy cream
1–2 tarragon sprigs, chopped, plus extra for garnish
squeeze of lemon juice, to taste

shallot stock   Heat the butter in a pan over a low heat. Add the shallots, garlic, and thyme, then cover and sweat gently until soft but not colored, 5–7 minutes. Add the stock and simmer for 15 minutes. Remove from the heat and let infuse for 15 minutes. Discard the garlic and thyme; measure 1 cup stock. (Any remaining shallot stock can be frozen.)

caramelized onions   Melt the butter with the garlic clove in a heavy-based frying pan, then add the onions with a pinch of salt. Cook over a very low heat, stirring occasionally, until the onions are very soft and caramelized, 45–60 minutes. When finished they should be deep golden in color, with a sweet, rich taste. Season and discard the garlic. Let cool.

for the tart bases   Preheat the oven to 425°F. Roll out the pastry to ⅛-inch thickness and cut out four 5-inch disks. Prick the disks evenly with a fork and place on a baking sheet lined with parchment paper. Spoon the caramelized onions on top of the pastry and spread out to a thin, even layer, leaving a ¼-inch clear border. Sprinkle with the thyme, if using. Lightly brush the pastry border with the egg wash. Bake until the pastry edges are risen and evenly golden, 12–16 minutes. Carefully transfer the tarts to a wire rack.

mushroom topping   While the tart bases are in the oven, halve or slice any larger mushrooms. Heat 4 tbsp butter in a frying pan over a medium heat until just foaming. Add the garlic and mushrooms and cook until lightly golden, 2–3 minutes. Season with salt and pepper. Add the 1 cup shallot stock and bubble to reduce by two-thirds. Add the cream, then stir in the remaining cold butter, a piece at a time. Stir in the chopped tarragon and a squeeze of lemon juice; check the seasoning and discard the garlic.

to assemble   Place the warm tart bases on warmed plates. Spoon the mushrooms on top, piling them up in the middle. Spoon the sauce over and garnish with tarragon.

as a main course Bake 2 rather than
4 pastry disks, making them larger. Pan-fry a 3-lb
chicken "crown" (i.e. legs removed) in a little oil
until well browned, then roast at 450°F until
cooked through, about 20 minutes. Let rest for
10 minutes, then carve each breast horizontally
into thick slices. Halve the pastry disks and place
on warmed plates. Spoon on the mushrooms,
mushroom sauce, and chicken. Garnish with
tarragon and serve with garlic purée (page 136).

Rutabaga & potato gratin with pine nuts

SERVES 4

3/4 cup pine nuts

1 cup milk

1¼ cups heavy cream

1 rosemary sprig

1 thyme sprig, plus extra for
garnish

4 garlic cloves, peeled

1 tbsp butter

2 rutabagas, each about 10oz

1 or 2 large baking potatoes, about
1lb in total

salt

toasting the pine nuts   Preheat the oven to 375°F. Scatter the pine nuts on a baking sheet and bake until lightly golden, 4–5 minutes.

infusing the creamy milk   Pour the milk and cream into a large saucepan and add the rosemary, thyme, garlic, and a third of the pine nuts. Place over a low heat to infuse for 20 minutes. Remove from the heat, cover, and let infuse for 30 minutes longer. Strain the creamy milk, discarding the pine nuts, garlic, and herbs.

preparing the gratin   Grease a medium to small, 2-inch-deep baking dish with the butter. Peel the rutabaga and potatoes, then cut lengthwise into ⅛-inch slices, using a mandoline or a sharp knife. Arrange a layer of rutabaga slices in the bottom of the prepared dish, drizzle with a little of the creamy milk, and add a pinch of salt. Cover with a layer of potato slices, and add a little more creamy milk and a sprinkling of salt. Continue alternating the layers in this way until the dish is almost full, then finish with a layer of creamy milk.

to bake   Cover the dish with foil and bake until the gratin is cooked through, 50–60 minutes. Test by inserting a metal skewer or a small knife in the center; it should meet with little resistance. Remove the foil and bake until the top layer is tinged golden brown, about 10 minutes longer. Let stand for 10–15 minutes before serving.

to serve   Spoon a neat portion of gratin onto each warmed plate and sprinkle with the remaining toasted pine nuts. Garnish with thyme sprigs.

note   This gratin is an excellent accompaniment for chicken, duck, and game, including venison.

Terrine of herb-cooked leeks & crab salad

SERVES 8

terrine

*8 cups vegetable nage (page 156),
 prepared a day in advance*

small bunch of tarragon

5 thyme sprigs

3 tbsp unsalted butter

salt and pepper

12 large leeks, white part only

crab salad

2/3 cup crab meat in pieces

3 tbsp mayonnaise

1 tbsp chopped chives

squeeze of lemon juice, to taste

to finish

4 vine-ripened tomatoes, sliced

cooking the leeks   Bring the vegetable nage to a simmer in a large pan with the tarragon, thyme, butter, and seasoning. Let infuse over a very low heat for 15 minutes. Add the leeks to the nage and cover with a disk of parchment paper that fits snugly in the pan. Simmer gently until the leeks are tender, 15–20 minutes. Remove from the heat and let the leeks cool in the liquid. When they are cool, remove with a slotted spoon and drain on paper towels.

preparing the terrine   Line an 8- by 3-inch terrine mold or loaf pan with plastic wrap, leaving an overhang of 4–5 inches all around. Put a layer of leeks in the bottom of the mold and press down firmly. Continue to layer the leeks in the mold until all of them have been used. Fold the overhanging plastic wrap over the leeks and top with a small tray or plate that just fits inside the mold. Place a couple of wrapped sticks of butter (or something similar) on top to press the terrine lightly. Refrigerate overnight.

crab salad   Put the crab meat into a bowl and fold in the mayonnaise, chopped chives, and lemon juice to taste.

to serve   Carefully remove the leek terrine from the mold and cut into 1/2-inch-thick slices, using a very sharp knife. Peel away the plastic wrap from the edges of each slice, then arrange the slices on serving plates or a large platter. Top with the crab salad and tomato slices.

as a main course   Serve the terrine with tea-smoked salmon or poached salmon and the crab salad. Tea-smoke 6 salmon fillets, about 5oz each, following the instructions on page 92. Or, poach the salmon fillets gently in fish stock with a slice of lemon added until just cooked. Let the salmon cool, then serve with the sliced leek terrine and the crab salad.

Anchovy & tomato terrine with basil purée

SERVES 8–10

20 large, vine-ripened tomatoes,
*   peeled, seeded and cut into*
*   quarters*
olive oil for drizzling
salt
1 tsp confectioners' sugar
3 garlic cloves, peeled and thinly
*   sliced*
small bunch of thyme
3 1/2 sheets of leaf gelatin
1 cup vegetable nage (page 156),
*   see note*
8oz white anchovies in oil,
*   drained*
bunch of basil (about 40 leaves),
*   stems removed*
basil oil (see page 47) for serving

tomato "petals"   Preheat the oven to 250°F. Arrange the tomato quarters on a baking sheet lined with parchment paper. Drizzle with a little olive oil and dust lightly with salt and the confectioners' sugar. Scatter the sliced garlic and thyme sprigs over the tomatoes. Put into the oven to dry until the tomatoes are deep red in color and very wrinkled, 3–4 hours. When ready, pick out the tomato "petals" and set aside.

the jellied nage   Soak the gelatin leaves in cold water to cover for 15 minutes. Warm 1/4 cup of the vegetable nage in a small saucepan until hot, then remove from the heat. Squeeze out excess water from the soaked gelatin sheets, then add them to the hot liquid and stir to melt. Stir in the remaining nage and let cool.

assembling the terrine   Line an 8- by 3-inch terrine mold or loaf pan with two layers of plastic wrap, leaving plenty overhanging the rim. Pour in a little of the jellied nage to cover the bottom thinly. Arrange a layer of tomato "petals" in the mold, followed by a layer of anchovies and then a sprinkling of basil leaves. Spoon a little of the jellied nage over the top. Repeat these layers to use up all of the ingredients. Fold the overlapping plastic wrap over and press firmly. Top with a small tray or plate that just fits inside the mold. Put a couple of wrapped sticks of butter (or something similar) on top to press the terrine lightly. Refrigerate overnight.

to serve   Unmold the terrine onto a serving plate and remove the plastic wrap. Streak the plate with the basil oil. Cut the terrine into slices with a warm knife.

note   If you happen to have any gazpacho consommé (page 105) on hand, use this in place of the herb nage—the flavor is sublime.

Blinis topped with curried oysters

Illustrated on page 112

Illustrated on page 112

SERVES 6–8

blinis
1lb firm, waxy potatoes
salt
1 tbsp all-purpose flour
1¹/2 tbsp crème fraîche (at room
   temperature)
1 tbsp chopped chives
1 tbsp chopped dill
1 egg, plus 2 egg yolks

curry sauce
4 tbsp butter
2 shallots, peeled and finely sliced
1 cup finely sliced bulb fennel
¹/4 cup white wine
1 cup fish or vegetable stock
2 tbsp crème fraîche
1 tsp medium curry powder
squeeze of lemon juice, to taste

to assemble
1 tbsp vegetable oil
2 tbsp butter
20–24 large, fresh oysters in shell,
   shucked (see page 48)
¹/2 cup cilantro leaves

blini batter   Put the potatoes into a medium pan, cover with cold water, and add salt. Bring to a simmer and simmer until tender, about 20 minutes. Drain the potatoes, then peel while still hot, using a small knife. Press them through a fine sieve or potato ricer. Measure 2 cups and put into a large bowl. Add the flour to the warm potato and whisk until smooth, then whisk in the crème fraîche and chopped herbs. Finally, add the whole egg and extra yolks and continue to whisk until the mixture is very smooth. Cover the bowl and let the batter rest for at least 15 minutes.

curry sauce   Melt half of the butter in a small pan. Add the shallots and fennel with a pinch of salt and stir, then cover and sweat gently until soft but not colored, about 10 minutes. Add the white wine to the pan and bubble to reduce by two-thirds. Add the stock, crème fraîche, and curry powder, and simmer over a low heat for 5 minutes. Remove from the heat, strain through a fine sieve, and set aside until ready to use.

to cook the blinis   Heat a large, nonstick frying pan over a medium heat. Add the oil and then the butter, and heat until melted and light brown in color. Cook the blinis in batches, 5 or 6 at a time: Drop tablespoonfuls of the batter into the pan, spacing them well apart, and cook until golden brown, about 1 minute on each side. Drain on paper towels and keep warm while cooking the rest. You should have enough batter for 20–24 blinis.

to finish   Bring the curry sauce back to a boil, add the oysters, and simmer for 1 minute. Arrange 3 blinis on each warmed plate. Using a slotted spoon, lift the oysters out of the sauce, and set one on each blini. Put the curry sauce back on a high heat and whisk in the remaining 2 tbsp butter in pieces. Add a squeeze of lemon juice and check the seasoning. Spoon the curry sauce over and around the blinis, and top with the cilantro leaves.

as a canapé   *Illustrated on page 113*
Make smaller blinis, using 2 tsp batter for each, and cook as above. Cut in half and sandwich together with different fillings. Try the following: prosciutto and soft cream cheese; blue cheese garnished with chervil or parsley; smoked salmon with crème fraîche and a little salmon caviar.

Creamed salt cod & celery root soup

SERVES 6

2oz salt cod

5 tbsp unsalted butter

1 onion, peeled and finely diced

1 garlic clove, peeled and crushed

1½ cups peeled and roughly diced celery root

3 cups chicken stock (page 156)

1 cup heavy cream

salt and pepper

1 tbsp chopped chives

preparing the salt cod   Soak the salt cod 24 hours in advance, using plenty of cold water to remove excess salt.

softening the vegetables   Melt the butter in a medium saucepan over a low heat. Add the onion and garlic, then cover and sweat, stirring occasionally, until soft, about 15 minutes. Add the diced celery root and sweat until softened, 5–7 minutes longer.

making the soup   Drain the salt cod and add to the vegetables along with the stock and cream. Bring to a simmer and simmer gently for about 15 minutes. Remove from the heat and let cool slightly, then purée in a blender until very smooth. Pass the soup through a fine sieve into a bowl and check the seasoning. Let cool, then chill thoroughly.

to finish   Serve in chilled bowls, sprinkled with chopped chives. Accompany with soft bread.

note   This soup can be served hot, if you prefer. It is also an excellent base for a chowder. Simply poach filleted chunks of fresh fish, such as cod or haddock, in the puréed soup until cooked, 6–8 minutes.

Crab croquettes with tomato dipping sauce

SERVES 6

croquette mix
1/2lb baking potatoes
salt and pepper
2 tbsp unsalted butter
1lb fresh flaked crab meat
2 egg yolks
*small bunch of dill, leaves stripped
   and chopped*

tomato dipping sauce
2 very ripe plum tomatoes, diced
1/2 small red onion, finely chopped
juice of 1/2 lemon
4 tbsp fine quality olive oil
2 tbsp chopped basil or marjoram

to finish
oil for deep-frying
flour for dusting
1 egg, beaten with a little water
2 cups dry bread crumbs
coarse sea salt
basil leaves for garnish

the croquette mix   Peel and quarter the potatoes. Put into a pan, add cold salted water to cover, and bring to a boil. Cook until tender, 15–20 minutes, then drain thoroughly. Leave, uncovered, for 3–4 minutes to dry off excess moisture. While still warm, push the potatoes through a sieve or potato ricer into a large bowl. Mix in the butter, followed by the crab meat, egg yolks, and chopped dill. Season with salt and pepper to taste. Let cool. When cold, roll the mixture into 8-inch-long cylinders about 3/4 inch in diameter. Place on a lightly floured tray and refrigerate for 1 hour.

tomato dipping sauce   Combine the diced tomatoes and red onion in a small bowl. Add the lemon juice, olive oil, and chopped basil. Toss to mix and season with salt and pepper to taste. Set aside to infuse at room temperature for 30 minutes.

to fry the croquettes   Heat oil for deep frying in a deep-fryer or other suitable pan to 350°F. Cut each cylinder into 3 equal lengths. Roll each one in flour to dust, then dip in egg wash, and, finally, roll in the bread crumbs to coat evenly all over. Deep-fry the croquettes, a few at a time, until golden brown, about 2 minutes. Drain on paper towels, season with sea salt, and keep warm while cooking the rest.

to serve   Arrange the croquettes on serving plates and spoon a portion of tomato dipping sauce alongside. Or, put them on a large platter with the dipping sauce in a serving bowl. Garnish with basil leaves.

variation   Shape the croquette mixture into cakes. Dust with flour, dip in egg wash, and coat with bread crumbs, then cook as above. Serve in split buns with lettuce leaves and tartar sauce, as a tasty snack or light meal.

Home-cured salmon with grainy mustard dressing

SERVES 8–10

1 very fresh salmon fillet, skin on, about 2¼lb

cure

3 cups rock salt

¾ cup sugar

grated zest of 3 lemons

grated zest of 3 limes

2 star anise, crushed or roughly ground

1½ cups chopped mixed herbs, such as dill, tarragon, and chives

mustard dressing

2 tbsp wholegrain mustard

1 tbsp sugar

1½ tbsp white wine vinegar

5 tbsp peanut or vegetable oil

1 tsp minced dill

salt and pepper

to finish

lemon wedges

dill sprigs

rye bread

curing the salmon   This needs to be done a day in advance. Lay the salmon fillet on a board and check for any small pin bones, removing them with tweezers. In a bowl, mix together the rock salt, sugar, citrus zests, crushed star anise, and 5 tbsp chopped herbs. Line a tray with plastic wrap, leaving plenty of overhang, and spread the curing mix on top. Place the salmon, flesh-side down, on the curing mix, and press so that it adheres. Turn to coat the other side. Wrap tightly in the plastic wrap and refrigerate for 24 hours, turning the salmon over after 12 hours.

the next day   Unwrap the salmon and rinse off the curing mix under cold running water. Pat dry with paper towels. Lay the fish skin-side down on a large, clean piece of plastic wrap. Scatter the remaining chopped herbs over the salmon to coat evenly, and press firmly. Wrap tightly in the plastic wrap, pressing the herbs into the fish, and refrigerate for 2 hours.

mustard dressing   Mix the mustard, sugar, and wine vinegar together in a bowl. Slowly drizzle in the oil, whisking to emulsify, then stir in the minced dill and season with salt and pepper to taste. Pour into a small serving dish.

to serve   Remove the plastic wrap from the salmon and place it on an oblong serving platter with the lemon wedges and the mustard dressing alongside. Garnish with dill sprigs. Cut the salmon into thin slices and accompany with rye bread.

as a canapé   Serve small slices of home-cured salmon on warm blinis or small rounds of pumpernickel bread, with a touch of crème fraîche and a sprinkling of snipped chives.

Honey-glazed ham with celery root rémoulade

SERVES 4–6

1 small, unsmoked ham hock,
  about 2¼lb
1 onion, peeled and chopped
1 carrot, peeled and chopped
1 celery stalk, trimmed and
  chopped
4 garlic cloves, peeled
3 bay leaves
1 thyme sprig
1 parsley sprig
2 cinnamon sticks
10 whole cloves
5 peppercorns

glaze
20 whole cloves
¼ cup port
¼ cup honey
1 tbsp Demerara sugar

celery root rémoulade
½ head celery root
4 tbsp mayonnaise (page 157)
squeeze of lemon juice
½ tbsp chopped parsley
salt and pepper

to cook the ham   Put the ham hock into a large pot and cover with cold water. Slowly bring to a boil, then drain off the water. Cover with fresh cold water, bring to a boil, and skim. Add the vegetables, garlic, herbs, and spices. Simmer gently, skimming frequently, until the meat is very tender, about 3 hours; it should be almost falling from the bone. Remove from the heat and let the ham cool in the liquid for 30 minutes.

to glaze the ham   Preheat the oven to 425°F. Remove the ham hock from the liquid and place on a board. Carefully remove the outer skin with a sharp knife. Score the fat layer in a trellis pattern, then stud with the cloves and place in a shallow roasting pan. Warm the port and honey together in a small pan, stirring until blended, then bring to a boil. Pour evenly over the ham and sprinkle with the Demerara sugar. Bake until the surface is glazed a rich golden brown, 15–20 minutes. Transfer to a plate and let cool.

celery root rémoulade   Peel the celery root and cut into julienne or matchstick strips. Put into a bowl with the mayonnaise, lemon juice, and chopped parsley, and toss to mix. Season with salt and pepper to taste. Set aside until ready to serve.

to serve   Carve the ham into thin slices and arrange on a platter or individual plates. Serve with the celery root rémoulade and accompany with thin slices of brown bread.

Oxtail & lentil ragout with root vegetables

SERVES 4

braised oxtail

1lb oxtail, cut into 2-inch lengths
salt and pepper
2–3 tbsp vegetable oil
1 carrot, peeled and cut into
  quarters
1 onion, peeled and cut into
  quarters
2 garlic cloves, peeled and cracked
2 cups red wine
4 cups chicken stock (page 156)
few thyme sprigs
1 bay leaf
5 black peppercorns

lentils

1 cup lentilles de Puy (or other
  green lentils)
1 carrot, peeled and quartered
1 onion, peeled and quartered
2 celery stalks, trimmed and
  chopped
2 garlic cloves, peeled and cracked
handful of thyme sprigs

to finish

4 tbsp unsalted butter, chilled and
  diced
2oz smoked Canadian bacon,
  diced
1 shallot, peeled and finely diced
3–4 tbsp chopped parsley

braised oxtail   Season the oxtail pieces with salt and pepper. Heat the oil in a large saucepan over a high heat, add the oxtail pieces, and sear on all sides until browned all over. Remove with a slotted spoon; set aside. Add the carrot, onion, and garlic to the pan and cook gently until softened and golden. Return the oxtail and add the wine. Bubble to reduce by two-thirds, then add the stock, thyme, bay leaf, and peppercorns. Bring back to a simmer and simmer gently, skimming occasionally, until the meat comes away from the bone easily, about 3 1/2 hours. Let the oxtail cool in the liquid. When cool, strain, reserving the liquid, but discarding the flavorings. Take the oxtail meat off the bone and shred the meat. Keep the meat and liquid to one side until ready to finish the dish.

to cook the lentils   Put the lentils into a saucepan, add cold water to cover, and bring to a boil. Drain and return to the pan. Repeat this process once more. Then add the vegetables, garlic, and thyme, and cover again with water. Bring to a boil, lower the heat, and simmer until the lentils are tender but still firm, 6–8 minutes. Remove from the heat and let cool in the liquid, then drain. Separate the vegetables from the lentils and chop these roughly; discard the garlic.

to finish   Heat 2 tbsp of the butter in a frying pan, add the bacon, and fry until golden. Add the shallot and fry gently for 1 minute, then add the shredded oxtail, 1 1/4 cups of the reserved oxtail liquid, the lentils, and chopped vegetables. Bring to a boil and bubble to reduce the liquid by half. Lower the heat and stir in the remaining butter. The consistency should be soupy. Sprinkle on the chopped parsley and ladle into warmed bowls.

as a main course   This dish is an excellent winter main course. Simply double the quantities and leave the oxtail on the bone after braising. Serve with creamy mash.

as a canapé   Cut small bread rounds, 1 inch in diameter, and toast to make croûtons. Top each one with a teaspoonful of oxtail ragout and serve hot.

Beef bourguignonne tartlets

SERVES 4

beef bourguignonne
1lb beef shank or cheek (or
    flank steak)
1 large carrot, peeled and halved
    lengthwise
1 large onion, peeled and
    quartered
2 celery stalks, halved
4 garlic cloves, peeled and
    crushed
2 bay leaves
handful of thyme sprigs
1¾ cups red wine
3 tbsp unsalted butter
2oz smoked Canadian bacon, cut
    into cubes
2 cups sliced button mushrooms
salt and pepper
1 chicken bouillon cube, crumbled

caramelized onions
4 tbsp unsalted butter
2 large onions, peeled and thinly
    sliced
2 garlic cloves, peeled and
    crushed

tartlet shells
1 quantity basic short pastry
    (page 156)
baby spinach or chard leaves,
    freshly wilted, for garnish

marinating the beef   This needs to be done a day ahead. Cut the meat roughly into 1½-inch cubes and put into a bowl with the carrot, onion, celery, garlic, bay leaves, thyme sprigs, and red wine. Cover and let marinate in the fridge overnight.

the bourguignonne base   The next day, strain off the wine and reserve. Tip the meat and vegetables onto paper towels, separating them (keeping the herbs with the vegetables), and pat dry; set aside. Melt 1 tbsp butter in a large frying pan over a medium heat, add the bacon, and fry until golden, 3–4 minutes. Remove with a slotted spoon and drain on paper towels; set aside. Melt another 1 tbsp butter in the frying pan, then add the reserved vegetables along with the mushrooms and fry until soft and golden, 7–8 minutes. Drain on paper towels and season with a pinch of salt.

cooking the beef bourguignonne   Put the frying pan back on the heat. Season the beef cubes with salt and pepper. Add the remaining 1 tbsp butter to the hot pan and, when it is very hot, add the beef cubes. Sear them, turning, until browned on all sides, 4–5 minutes. Put the beef into a casserole or heavy-based pan with the vegetables, bacon, bouillon cube, and wine. Bring to a simmer and cook gently, skimming as necessary, until the meat is very tender, falling easily into strands, and the liquid is reduced right down, about 3 hours. Add a little water during cooking, if necessary. Let cool, then discard the vegetables and herbs. Break up the meat with a wooden spoon.

caramelized onions   Heat a large frying pan over a medium heat and add the butter. When foaming, add the onions and garlic, and season with a pinch of salt. Cook slowly until soft and caramelized to a rich golden brown, 30–45 minutes. Drain and set aside to cool.

tarts   Preheat the oven to 425°F. Roll out the short pastry and cut out four 6-inch disks. Use to line individual tartlet molds, trimming away excess pastry. Prick the bases with a fork. Divide the caramelized onions evenly among the pastry shells. Bake the tarts until crisp and golden brown, 12–15 minutes. Meanwhile, gently reheat the bourguignonne. Spoon the meat into the pastry shells and garnish with warm spinach or chard.

as a main course
Cook double the quantity of bourguignonne until the meat is tender, but don't break it up after cooking. Cut 4 rectangles of puff pastry, about 5 by 3 inches, score them with a knife, and lay on a baking sheet. Bake at 425°F until crisp and golden, 12–15 minutes. Serve each bourguignonne portion topped with a puff pastry rectangle and accompanied by broccoli and haricots vert.

as a main course Triple the quantities: You will need a boned and rolled short saddle of lamb, weighing about 2¼lb. Roast the meat as above, allowing 30–40 minutes, then let rest for 10 minutes. Carve the meat into thick slices and arrange on warmed plates Serve with the minted peas and roasted new potatoes, omitting the Parmesan. Garnish with mint leaves.

Roasted lamb cannelloni with minted peas

SERVES 6

2 boneless lamb sirloins, about 1lb

salt and pepper

1 tbsp olive oil

2 tbsp unsalted butter

1 carrot, peeled and roughly chopped

1 onion, peeled and roughly chopped

1 thyme sprig

1 rosemary sprig

1 cup shelled green peas

2 shallots, peeled and minced

½ cup mint leaves, roughly chopped

to finish

2oz Parmesan cheese, finely pared into shavings

to cook the lamb   Preheat the oven to 425°F. Season the lamb all over with salt and pepper. Heat a medium, stovetop-to-oven frying pan (with a metal handle) or casserole over a high heat. Add the olive oil followed by 1 tbsp of butter and heat until golden brown. Add the lamb and let it color for 1 minute, then turn to color the other sides lightly. Remove the meat from the pan and set aside. Add the carrot, onion, thyme, and rosemary to the pan, then set the meat on top of the vegetables. Transfer to the oven and roast for 8–10 minutes for medium-rare meat. Let rest in a warm place for 10 minutes.

minted peas   Add the peas to a pan of boiling water and simmer until tender, about 3 minutes. Drain and toss with the remaining 1 tbsp butter, the shallots, and chopped mint. Season with salt and pepper to taste.

to serve   Using a very sharp knife, cut the lamb into very thin slices. Lay one slice flat on a board and season lightly with salt and pepper, then add a spoonful of peas, scattering them along the width. Roll the meat around the peas and secure with a toothpick. Repeat to use all the lamb slices. Arrange on individual plates, or a platter. Scatter any remaining peas on top and sprinkle with Parmesan shavings.

posh

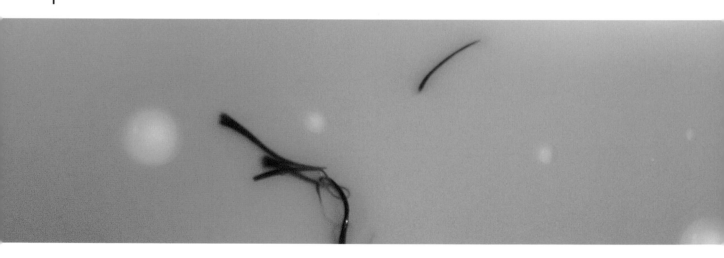

Asparagus tagliatelle with morel cream & chervil

Truffle & white bean soup

Lime-marinated scallop ceviche

Roasted scallops with asparagus & parsnip sauce

Creamed leeks with langoustines

Langoustines with garlic purée

Crab with avocado & sesame phyllo wafers

Crab & salmon tortellini in ginger crab bisque

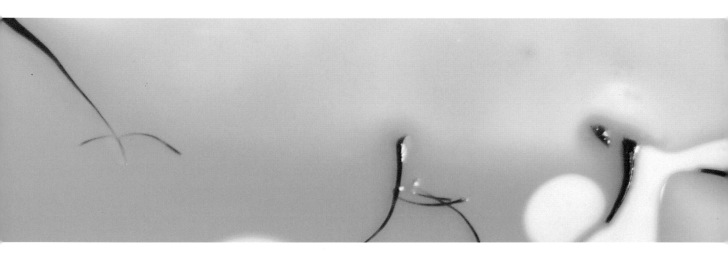

Red mullet on fennel with vanilla & olive sauce

Roasted quail, cabbage & chanterelle soup

Chicken with cèpe & artichoke carpaccio

Breast of squab with beet vinaigrette

Terrine of foie gras, squab & ham hock

Foie gras poached in sauternes with peas

Open ravioli of rabbit with mustard sauce

Seared veal carpaccio

Asparagus tagliatelle with morel cream & chervil

SERVES 4

asparagus tagliatelle

12–16 thick asparagus spears

morel cream

1½oz dried morels, or other dried
*   wild mushrooms*

4 tsp unsalted butter

3 shallots, peeled and finely diced

3 garlic cloves, peeled and cracked

salt and pepper

2/3 cup rich Madeira

¼ cup heavy cream

squeeze of lemon juice, to taste

1 tbsp tarragon leaves, chopped

16 small chervil sprigs

to soak the dried morels   Bring 3 cups water to a boil in a pan, then add the dried mushrooms and remove from the heat. Cover and let soak until the mushrooms are soft, about 45 minutes. Drain, reserving the liquid.

tagliatelle   Trim the woody stalk ends from the asparagus spears and peel the lower ends of the stalks. Slice the asparagus lengthwise, using a mandoline or swivel vegetable peeler, into very thin strips to make "tagliatelle." Cover with plastic wrap and refrigerate until needed.

morel cream   Melt the butter in a medium pan over a low heat and add the shallots and garlic with a pinch of salt. Stir, then cover and sweat gently, stirring occasionally, until the shallots are soft and translucent but not colored, about 10 minutes. Add the Madeira, increase the heat to medium-high, and bubble to reduce by two-thirds. Add the softened mushrooms, 5 tbsp of the reserved mushroom liquid, the cream, and another pinch of salt. Bring to a simmer and let the sauce bubble gently for 5–7 minutes to reduce and thicken slightly. Check that the mushrooms have softened sufficiently. If not, add another tbsp mushroom water and simmer for 1–2 minutes longer. When ready, remove from the heat and check the seasoning. Add a squeeze of lemon juice and stir in the chopped tarragon. Keep warm until ready to serve.

to serve   Add the asparagus tagliatelle to a pan of boiling salted water and blanch for 2 minutes. Drain thoroughly and arrange on warmed plates. Spoon the morel cream over and around the asparagus. Scatter the sprigs of chervil on top.

note   When in season, use fresh morels instead of dried; you will need about 4oz. Clean thoroughly, but do not soak. Sauté lightly in a little butter before adding to the shallots.

Truffle & white bean soup

SERVES 6

*½ cup dried white beans, soaked
   in cold water overnight*
1 whole garlic bulb
1 onion, peeled and quartered
1 carrot, peeled and quartered
*1 sprig each of rosemary, thyme,
   and parsley*
7-oz piece slab bacon
8 cups chicken stock (page 156)
7 tbsp unsalted butter
4 shallots, peeled and minced
1 lemon thyme sprig
⅔ cup heavy cream
*1 tbsp truffle oil, plus extra
   for drizzling*

to cook the beans   Drain the soaked beans, put them into a large pot, and cover with fresh cold water. Bring to a boil, then drain and return the beans to the pan. Cut the garlic bulb in half crosswise (through the cloves) and add one half to the pan along with the onion, carrot, rosemary, thyme, and parsley. Roughly chop half of the bacon and add to the pan. Pour in the stock and bring to a simmer, then cook until the beans are tender, 1½–2 hours. Drain the beans, reserving the cooking liquid. Discard the bacon, herb sprigs, vegetables, and garlic. Skim excess fat from the liquid.

the soup base   Peel and mince the other half of the garlic. Dice the remaining bacon. Melt 5 tbsp of the butter in a large pan and add the minced garlic, diced bacon, shallots, and lemon thyme. Stir, then cover and sweat over a low heat until the shallots are soft but not colored, about 15 minutes.

the puréed soup   Add the reserved bean cooking liquid to the soup base, along with half of the beans and the cream. Simmer gently for 15 minutes, then remove from the heat. Let cool slightly, then tip into a blender and blend until smooth. Pass through a fine sieve into a clean pan or bowl. Adjust the seasoning, then stir in the truffle oil. (The soup can be prepared ahead to this stage and kept in the fridge for up to 2 days; refrigerate the whole beans separately.)

to serve   Melt the remaining 2 tbsp butter in a medium pan, add the remaining whole beans, and warm through. Heat the soup in a separate pan. Spoon the hot buttery beans into the center of 6 warmed serving bowls and pour the hot puréed soup over them to cover. Finish with droplets of truffle oil.

as a canapé Serve small portions in demitasse cups. Halve the quantities for 8–10 canapé-sized portions. Just before pouring into the cups, blend the soup using an immersion blender to froth it. Top with a sprinkling of chopped chives.

Lime-marinated scallop ceviche

SERVES 4

8 sea scallops

sea salt

marinade

1/4 English cucumber

*2 vine-ripened tomatoes, peeled,
    seeded, and diced*

1 tbsp finely diced shallot

finely grated zest of 1 lime

juice of 1–2 limes

4 tbsp fish or vegetable stock

1 tsp sugar

10 basil leaves, chopped

10 cilantro leaves, roughly torn

2/3 cup extra virgin olive oil

preparing the scallops   Chill 4 deep serving plates in the fridge for 20 minutes. Meanwhile, slice each scallop horizontally into 4 thin rounds. Arrange 8 slices on each of the chilled plates. Lightly season the scallops with a little sea salt.

preparing the marinade   Peel the cucumber, halve lengthwise, and scoop out the seeds, then cut the flesh into small dice. Put into a bowl with the tomatoes. Add the shallot, lime zest, the juice of 1 lime, the stock, sugar, herbs, and olive oil. Adjust the sweet and sour balance, adding a little extra lime juice or sugar to taste.

to marinate   Spoon the marinade evenly over the scallops. Cover the plates with plastic wrap and let marinate at cool room temperature for 15 minutes.

to serve   Uncover the scallop ceviche and check the seasoning.

Roasted scallops with asparagus & parsnip sauce

SERVES 4

12 asparagus spears

8–12 sea scallops

salt and pepper

3 tbsp olive oil

1 tbsp unsalted butter

squeeze of lemon juice

parsnip sauce

1 tsp cumin seeds

6oz parsnips

1 tbsp unsalted butter

1¼ cups chicken stock (page 156)

¼ cup heavy cream

parsnip sauce   Make this first. Heat a small frying pan until hot, then add the cumin seeds and toast until lightly colored, 45–60 seconds. Tip onto a board and crush with the back of a heavy knife. Peel the parsnips, quarter lengthwise, and remove the woody cores, then roughly chop. Melt the butter in a pan and add the parsnips and cumin. Stir, then cover and sweat until very soft, about 25 minutes. Add two-thirds of the stock, then stir in the cream and bring to a simmer. Cook gently for 5 minutes, then transfer to a blender and blend until very smooth, adding a little more stock if necessary to achieve a pourable consistency. Pass through a fine sieve into a clean pan and set aside.

blanching the asparagus   Trim the woody ends from the asparagus and peel the lower end of the stalks. Add the asparagus to a pan of boiling salted water and blanch for 2–3 minutes. Drain and refresh in cold water.

sautéeing the scallops   Carefully cut each scallop in half horizontally into 2 disks and season with salt and pepper. Heat a large frying pan over a medium-high heat. When hot, add the olive oil and then the butter. When it is sizzling, add the scallop disks in a single layer and cook for 30 seconds. Turn and cook the other side for 30 seconds. Immediately remove and drain on paper towels, then sprinkle with a little lemon juice.

to assemble   While sautéeing the scallops, reheat the parsnip sauce and, if necessary, warm the asparagus briefly in the microwave. Arrange the scallops in the center of warmed plates, top with the asparagus, and spoon the parsnip sauce over. Serve immediately.

Creamed leeks with langoustines

SERVES 4

16 raw langoustines (scampi) or
 jumbo shrimp, shelled and
 deveined
2 large leeks (white part only)
salt and pepper
½ cup heavy cream
3 garlic cloves, peeled and cracked
4 tsp minced chives
lemon juice, to taste
2 tbsp olive oil
2 tbsp unsalted butter

preparing the langoustines   Rinse the langoustines, pat dry with paper towels, and set aside.

creamed leeks   Quarter the leeks lengthwise and slice finely. Add to a pan of boiling salted water and cook until tender, 3–4 minutes. Drain and refresh in ice water, then drain thoroughly. Put the cream, garlic, and leeks into a clean pan and bring to a simmer. Let bubble until reduced by about two-thirds to a rich, thick sauce; discard the garlic. Season with salt and pepper to taste, stir in the chives, and finish with a squeeze of lemon juice. Set the creamed leeks aside; keep warm.

sautéeing the langoustines   Heat a large, nonstick frying pan over a high heat. Season the langoustines with a little salt. When the pan is hot, add the olive oil and then the butter. When it is sizzling, add the langoustines and sauté quickly until golden brown, 1–2 minutes. Remove and drain on paper towels. Finish with a squeeze of lemon juice.

to serve   Spoon the leek sauce into the center of warmed serving plates. Top with the langoustines. Serve with slices of crusty baguette.

as individual tarts   Instead of langoustines use 16 cooked, shelled, small shrimp . Prepare the creamed leeks as above. Line four 4-inch tart molds with basic short pastry (page 156). Prick the bases with a fork, line with parchment paper and baking beans, cover, and let rest in the fridge for 30 minutes. Bake the tart shells at 400°F until golden brown and crisp, 15–20 minutes. Let firm up for a few minutes, then fill with the creamed leeks and top with the shrimp. Warm in the oven for 5–10 minutes before serving, if necessary.

Langoustines with garlic purée

SERVES 4

16 raw langoustines (scampi) or
   jumbo shrimp, shelled and
   deveined
salt and pepper
1 tbsp olive oil
4 tbsp butter
1 tsp chopped thyme
2 tsp sliced almonds
lemon juice, to taste

garlic purée
3 garlic bulbs
1 cup heavy cream

preparing the langoustines   Rinse the langoustines, pat dry with paper towels, and set aside.

garlic purée   Separate the garlic cloves, peel, and put into a small saucepan. Cover with cold water and bring to a boil, then drain; repeat this process three times, then return the garlic to the pan. Pour in the cream, add a pinch of salt, and bring to a slow simmer. Let bubble gently, stirring occasionally, until the cream is reduced and the garlic is soft. Tip into a blender and blend until smooth. Pass through a sieve into a bowl, check the seasoning, and keep warm.

to cook the langoustines   Heat a large, nonstick frying pan over a high heat. Season the langoustines with a little salt. When the pan is hot, add the olive oil and then the butter. When it is sizzling, add the langoustines and sauté quickly for 30 seconds. Add the thyme and almonds, and sauté until golden brown, about 1 minutes longer. Remove and drain on paper towels. Finish with a squeeze of lemon juice.

to serve   Arrange the langoustines with the thyme and almonds on warmed plates. Spoon the garlic purée into small serving bowls and place alongside for dipping. Serve immediately.

shrimp skewers   Instead of langoustines, use 20–24 raw tiger shrimp (deveined and heads removed). Thread the shrimp onto soaked wooden kabob skewers and sauté in olive oil, along with the thyme and almonds, until the shrimp turn pink, about 1 minute on each side. Serve the shrimp skewers with the pan juices spooned over, garnished with ramps or thyme sprigs. Accompany with the garlic purée.

Crab with avocado & sesame phyllo wafers

SERVES 4

14oz flaked crab meat

2 tsp olive oil

5 basil leaves, minced

20 cilantro leaves, minced

salt

tomato dressing

1 very ripe tomato

squeeze of lemon juice

2 tbsp olive oil

pinch of sugar

salt and pepper

sesame phyllo wafers

1–2 sheets of phyllo pastry,
  thawed if frozen

2 tbsp melted butter

1/3 cup sesame seeds, toasted

avocado crème fraîche

2 ripe avocados

1/4 cup crème fraîche

squeeze of lemon juice

to finish

frisée (pale leaves only)

small cilantro sprigs

crab meat   Put the crab meat into a bowl, checking that there are no small fragments of shell. Add the olive oil and minced herbs, toss to mix, and season with a little salt to taste.

tomato dressing   Cut the tomato in half and press through a fine sieve into a bowl; you should have about 1/4 cup clear, rosy tomato water. Add the lemon juice, olive oil, and sugar. Season with salt and pepper to taste. Cover and refrigerate.

sesame phyllo wafers   Preheat the oven to 375°F. Using a 2 1/2-inch metal cutter, cut 12 rounds from the phyllo pastry. Lay the phyllo rounds on a baking sheet lined with parchment paper. Lightly brush with butter and sprinkle with the toasted sesame seeds. Cover with another sheet of parchment, then invert another baking sheet on top to weigh it down. Bake until golden and crisp, 8–10 minutes. Carefully remove from the hot baking sheets and let the phyllo wafers cool on the paper.

avocado crème fraîche   Peel, halve, and pit the avocados, then roughly chop the flesh. Put into a blender with 4 tsp cold water and blend until smooth. Transfer to a bowl and fold in the crème fraîche. Add the lemon juice and season with salt to taste. Cover the surface closely with plastic wrap to prevent discoloration.

to assemble   Arrange little towers on serving plates, alternating the crab meat and avocado crème fraîche between sesame phyllo wafers. Top with a little pile of frisée and a few cilantro sprigs. Surround with a drizzle of tomato dressing.

Crab & salmon tortellini in ginger crab bisque

SERVES 8

bisque

14oz crab shells and/or shrimp
    shells, broken
2 tbsp olive oil
1/2 onion, peeled and roughly
    chopped
3 garlic cloves, peeled and cracked
2·oz piece fresh ginger, peeled and
    grated
1 carrot, peeled and roughly
    chopped
1/4 fennel bulb, roughly chopped
1 celery stalk, trimmed and
    roughly chopped
3–4 thyme sprigs
1 tsp fennel seeds
1 tsp coriander seeds
1 tbsp tomato paste
1 cup heavy cream
salt and pepper
lemon juice, to taste

tortellini

    wonton wrappers
1¼lb fresh salmon fillet, skinned
1/2 cup light cream
14oz flaked crab meat
20 basil leaves, chopped
1 egg yolk
juice of 1/2 lemon
1 quantity fresh pasta dough
    (page 157), or 10-oz package
1 egg, beaten with a little milk
    (egg wash)

preparing the bisque   Preheat the oven to 375°F. Put the shells into a roasting pan and roast for 6–8 minutes, then set aside to cool. Heat the olive oil in a large saucepan and add the onion, garlic, ginger, carrot, fennel, celery, thyme, and seeds. Stir, then cover and sweat gently until the vegetables soften, about 15 minutes. Stir in the tomato paste and cook for 1 minute, then add the roasted shells and 8 cups water. Bring to a simmer and gently simmer for 30 minutes, skimming occasionally. Strain the liquid into a clean pan and bring to a boil. Let bubble to reduce by two-thirds, to about 2 cups. Stir in the cream and bring back to a simmer. Strain again through a fine sieve. Season with salt and pepper, and add a squeeze of lemon juice to taste. Set aside until ready to serve.

tortellini filling   Chill your food processor bowl in the fridge. In the meantime, check the salmon for any small bones and remove with tweezers, then cut into 1/4-inch dice. Put 1 cup of the salmon into the chilled food processor bowl along with the cream and a pinch of salt. Blend for about 1 minute to a fine paste. Transfer to a mixing bowl and add the crab, remaining salmon, the basil, egg yolk, and lemon juice. Mix well to combine and season with salt and pepper.

shaping the tortellini   If using pasta, roll it thinly and cut into 4-inch squares; you will need 32 in total. Lay the pasta squares or wonton wrappers flat on a surface and put 1 tbsp of filling in the center of each one. Lightly brush the edges with egg wash, then fold 2 opposite corners to meet, to form triangles. Press out any trapped air and pinch the edges tightly to seal. Bring the other 2 corners together to form a cone and press the tips together.

cooking the tortellini   Add the tortellini to a large pan of boiling water, bring back to a boil, and cook for 1½ minutes.

to finish   While the tortellini are cooking, bring the bisque back to a simmer over a medium heat, then froth up with an immersion blender. Ladle into warmed bowls. Drain the tortellini and divide among the bowls. Serve at once.

note   The bisque can be served on its own without the tortellini.

Red mullet on fennel with vanilla & olive sauce

Illustrated on page 142

SERVES 4

*2 small fennel bulbs, about 7oz
  in total*

lemon juice, to taste

4 tbsp olive oil

salt and pepper

7 tbsp unsalted butter, chilled

20 green olives

½ vanilla bean, split lengthwise

*3 cups fish stock or vegetable nage
  (page 156)*

5 tbsp heavy cream

4 red mullet fillets, 4–5oz each

fennel salad   Trim the fennel, reserving a few feathery fronds for garnish if desired, and slice the bulbs thinly. Put one-fourth of the sliced fennel in a bowl with a squeeze of lemon juice and 2 tbsp of the olive oil. Toss to mix and season with salt and pepper. Cover and let marinate in the fridge for 40 minutes.

vanilla and olive sauce   Melt 5 tbsp butter in a small pan over a low heat. When hot, add the remaining fennel and stir, then cover and sweat over a low heat until very tender, about 15 minutes. Meanwhile, remove the pits from half of the olives and slice; set aside, reserving the pits. Scrape out the seeds from the vanilla bean and add to the pan with the empty pod, the whole olives, and reserved pits. Stir in the stock or nage and bring to a boil. Let bubble until reduced by half, about 20 minutes. Add the cream and simmer for 5 minutes longer. Pass the sauce through a fine sieve into a clean pan and add the sliced olives. Keep warm.

to cook the red mullet   Season the fillets on both sides with a little salt. Place a large, nonstick frying pan over a medium heat. When hot, add the remaining 2 tbsp olive oil. Place the fillets in the pan, skin-side down, and cook for 1½ minutes. Flip the fillets over and cook for 30 seconds longer. Remove and drain on paper towels, then finish with a squeeze of lemon juice.

to finish the sauce   While the red mullet is cooking, gently whisk the remaining 2 tbsp cold butter into the olive sauce, a piece at a time. Season with a little salt and add a squeeze of lemon juice to taste.

to serve   Drain the fennel salad of excess dressing, then arrange in the center of warmed serving plates. Place the red mullet fillets on top and dress with the vanilla and olive sauce. Garnish with fennel fronds, if desired.

as a main course   *Illustrated on page 143*

Buy 4 sea bass fillets, about 6oz each. Pan-fry, skin-side down first, for 3 minutes, then turn and cook on the other side for 30–60 seconds longer. Place on warmed plates with hot new potatoes and the fennel salad alongside. Dress the fish with the olive and vanilla sauce, and serve.

Roasted quail, cabbage & chanterelle soup

SERVES 4

chanterelle soup base
2 tbsp unsalted butter
2 shallots, peeled and finely sliced
2 thyme sprigs
2 tarragon sprigs, plus extra leaves
  for garnish
salt and pepper
2½ cups chicken stock (page 156)
4oz chanterelles or other wild
  mushrooms, cleaned

roast quail
4 quail, wings removed
2 tbsp vegetable oil
1 tsp unsalted butter

buttered cabbage
½ small head Savoy cabbage,
  outer leaves removed
4 tbsp butter

making the soup   Place a small saucepan over a low heat, add 1 tbsp of the butter, and heat until melted. Add the shallots along with the thyme, tarragon, and a pinch of salt. Stir, then cover and sweat gently until the shallots are soft, about 20 minutes. Pour in the stock and bring to a simmer. Meanwhile, heat a frying pan over a medium heat, add the remaining butter, and heat until melted. Add the mushrooms and sauté for 2 minutes, then remove and drain on paper towels. Add the mushrooms to the soup and simmer for 20 minutes longer, skimming as necessary. Check the seasoning and remove from the heat.

roasting the quail   While you are preparing the soup, preheat the oven to 450°F and season the quail with salt and pepper. Heat a stovetop-to-oven frying pan (with a metal handle) or casserole over a medium-high heat. Add the oil and, when it is smoking hot, add the butter and then the quail. Turn them, using tongs, until lightly caramelized all over. Transfer the pan to the oven and roast for 5–6 minutes for medium rare, or 8–10 minutes for well done. Transfer to a warm plate and let rest for 10 minutes.

buttered cabbage   Meanwhile, shred the cabbage into thin ribbons. Add to a pan of boiling salted water and cook until tender, 4–5 minutes. Immediately refresh in cold water and drain. Place a medium pan over a low heat, add the butter, and melt. Add the cabbage, along with a pinch of salt and pepper, and reheat gently for about 1 minute. Remove from the heat and keep warm.

to serve   Reheat the soup. Remove the quail legs and breasts from the bone (or leave on if serving whole). Place the hot buttered cabbage in the center of warmed soup plates and top with the quail. Ladle the soup around the cabbage and garnish with tarragon leaves.

Chicken with cèpe & artichoke carpaccio

SERVES 2

2 large globe artichokes

*1 quantity pickling marinade
(see page 10)*

*2 large cèpes (ideally with caps the
same size as the prepared
artichokes), cleaned*

1¼ cups olive oil

6 garlic cloves, peeled and cracked

3 thyme sprigs

2 bay leaves

*2 tbsp dried porcini or other dried
wild mushrooms*

salt and pepper

*1 small skinless boneless chicken
breast half, cut into wide strips*

4 tsp unsalted butter

juice of ½ lemon

about 20 tarragon leaves

pickled artichokes   Pull off the outer leaves from the artichokes to reveal the hearts, then remove the hairy choke from each one. Bring the pickling marinade to a simmer in a pan. Add the artichoke hearts and simmer until just tender, about 5 minutes. Remove from the heat and let cool in the marinade, then refrigerate until needed.

cèpe confit   Check that the cèpes are thoroughly cleaned, then set aside. Put the olive oil, garlic, thyme, bay leaves, and dried mushrooms into a pan that will be just large enough to take the cèpes too. Add a pinch of salt. Let infuse for 20 minutes over a very low heat; do not let the garlic color. Add the cèpes and ensure that they are completely submerged in the infused oil. Turn the heat up very slightly and "confit" the mushroom caps in the warm oil for 5–6 minutes. Remove the pan from the heat and let the cèpes cool in the oil.

sautéed chicken   Season the chicken strips with salt and pepper. Place a frying pan over a medium heat, then add the butter and heat until melted and lightly browned. Add the seasoned chicken and sauté until evenly colored and just cooked through, 3–4 minutes. Remove from the heat and keep warm.

the dressing   Lift the cèpes out of the oil with a slotted spoon and place on a board. Measure ½ cup of the confit oil and put into a small bowl with the lemon juice and tarragon leaves. Season with salt and pepper, and whisk to emulsify.

to assemble   Using a very sharp knife, cut the cèpes and artichokes into very fine slices. Arrange the slices, overlapping, on warmed plates. Place the chicken on top. Spoon the dressing over and serve at once.

Breast of squab with beet vinaigrette

SERVES 4

8 thin slices pancetta or bacon

8 boneless squab breasts

salt and pepper

4 tbsp butter

beet vinaigrette

1 medium beet, about 6oz

½ cup port

½ cup vegetable nage (page 156)

1 tbsp balsamic vinegar

¼ cup olive oil

squeeze of lemon juice

to finish

4oz baby beet leaves, baby red chard, or other small salad leaves

2 tbsp vinaigrette (page 157)

beet vinaigrette   Make this first. Peel the beet and cut into ⅛-inch-thick slices, then cut these slices into ⅛-inch cubes. Put into a small saucepan and add the port and nage to cover. Bring to a simmer and cook the beet until tender, 10–15 minutes. Remove the beet cubes with a slotted spoon and set aside on a plate. Let the cooking liquid bubble until reduced and thickened to a light syrupy consistency. Let cool. Add the cooked beet to the cooled liquid, along with the balsamic vinegar and olive oil. Add a squeeze of lemon juice and check the seasoning.

oven-crisped bacon   Preheat the oven to 400°F. Lay the pancetta slices side by side on a baking sheet lined with parchment paper. Cover with another sheet of paper and place another heavy baking sheet on top, to keep the pancetta slices flat. Cook in the oven until crisp, 8–12 minutes. Remove and drain on paper towels.

cooking the squab breasts   Season the squab breasts on both sides with salt and pepper. Heat a stovetop-to-oven frying pan (with a metal handle) or casserole over a high heat, then add the butter. Place the squab breasts, skin-side down, in the hot pan and cook until golden brown, about 2 minutes. Turn them over and cook for 1 minute longer. Transfer the pan to the oven and cook for 3–4 minutes for medium rare; 5–6 minutes for medium. Remove and let rest in a warm place for 5 minutes.

to serve   Gently warm the beet cubes in their liquid. Dress the salad leaves with the vinaigrette. Arrange 2 squab breasts, skin-side up, on each warmed plate. Spoon the warm beet cubes on top and drizzle the liquid over. Arrange the salad leaves and pancetta alongside.

as a canapé Lay slices of the foie gras terrine on toasted slices of brioche and cut into fingers. Skewer quartered pickled artichokes (page 10) onto toothpicks and press one into each canapé.

Terrine of foie gras, squab & ham hock

SERVES 8–10

jellied ham

1 ham hock, soaked overnight in cold water (in the fridge)

1 carrot, peeled and quartered

1 onion, peeled and quartered

1 leek (white only), quartered

1 celery stalk, trimmed and halved

2 garlic cloves, peeled and cracked

1 chicken bouillon cube

1–2 thyme sprigs

1½ sheets leaf gelatin

fois gras

1 fresh foie gras, about 1lb

½ cup port

2 tbsp Cognac

½ cup Madeira

squab breasts

4 squab breasts

salt and pepper

1 tsp vegetable oil

1 tbsp unsalted butter

for serving

coarse sea salt

cornichons

pear chutney (page 157), or other good, fruity chutney

to cook the ham hock   Put into a large pan, cover with cold water, and slowly bring to a boil, then drain. Cover generously with fresh cold water, bring to a boil, and skim, then add the vegetables, garlic, bouillon cube, and thyme. Simmer gently, skimming frequently, until the ham is very tender, about 3 hours. Let cool in the liquid for 30 minutes.

marinating the foie gras   Cut the foie gras into 1-inch slices and place in a bowl with the port, Cognac, and Madeira. Let marinate for 2 hours.

preparing the jellied ham   Lift out the warm ham, take the meat off the bone, and shred it; put into a bowl. Measure 1¼ cups of the cooking liquid into a pan and reduce by half. Meanwhile, soften the gelatin in cold water to cover for 15 minutes. Take the reduced liquid off the heat. Squeeze the gelatin leaves to remove excess water, then add to the liquid, stirring to melt. Pour over the shredded ham and stir, then let cool.

cooking the squab breasts   Preheat the oven to 400°F and season the squab breasts. Heat a stovetop-to-oven frying pan (with a metal handle) or casserole over a high heat. Add the oil, followed by the butter. Cook the squab breasts, skin-side down, in the hot pan for 2–3 minutes, then turn and cook on the other side for 1 minute. Transfer the pan to the oven and cook for 2–3 minutes for medium rare. Remove and let rest for 10 minutes, then slice each breast in half horizontally.

sautéeing the foie gras   Remove the foie gras from the marinade, pat dry with paper towels, and season. Heat a frying pan over a medium-high heat until very hot. Add the foie gras slices to the hot, dry pan and fry until golden, 1 minute on each side. Remove and let cool, then chill briefly.

the terrine   Line an 8- by 3-inch terrine mold or loaf pan with a double layer of plastic wrap, leaving an overhang. Put one-fourth of the ham in the bottom of the mold and press firmly. Cover with a third of the foie gras, then a third of the squab slices. Repeat these layers twice and finish with a layer of ham. Fold the plastic wrap over and place a small tray and something heavy on top to press the terrine. Refrigerate overnight.

to serve   Unmold the terrine. Cut into thick slices using a warm, sharp knife, then peel away the plastic wrap. Arrange a terrine slice on each plate. Sprinkle with coarse sea salt and serve with cornichons and chutney.

Foie gras poached in sauternes with peas

SERVES 4

⅓ cup shelled fresh peas

4 slices of foie gras, about 1 inch thick and 3oz each

salt and pepper

sweet wine poaching liquid

2¼lb chicken bones or wings, chopped

1 onion, peeled and roughly diced

½ cup peeled and roughly diced celery root,

1 celery stalk, trimmed and roughly chopped

½ leek, roughly chopped

2oz dried mushrooms

2 cups Sauternes or other similar sweet wine

sweet wine poaching liquid Prepare this in advance. Place the chicken bones or wings in a large pot and cover with plenty of cold water, about 2½ quarts. Bring to a boil and skim, then simmer, skimming frequently, for 20 minutes. Add the onion, celery root, celery, leek, and dried mushrooms, and gently simmer for 1½ hours, skimming as necessary. Remove from the heat and let cool for 30 minutes. Strain the stock through a cheesecloth-lined sieve into a clean pan; discard the bones and vegetables. Reduce, if necessary, over a medium-high heat to 4 cups. Pour half of the wine into a wide saucepan, bring to a boil, and bubble to reduce until almost syrupy. Add the rest of the wine and reduce again, by about two-thirds. Add the chicken stock to the sweet wine reduction and return to a simmer.

blanching the peas Add the peas to a pan of boiling water and blanch for 1 minute, then drain and refresh in cold water. Drain and set aside.

foie gras Heat a large frying pan over a high heat until very hot. Season both sides of the foie gras slices with salt, then fry them on one side only until nicely caramelized, about 30 seconds. Carefully transfer them to the gently simmering stock. Poach the foie gras for 3–4 minutes, adding the blanched peas 1 minute before the end.

to serve Very carefully lift the foie gras slices into warmed serving bowls. Taste the poaching liquid and adjust the seasoning. Pour the liquid over the foie gras, spooning in the peas too.

note You can use the poaching liquid as the basis for a delicious soup, without the foie gras. Try flavoring it with smoked Canadian bacon or smoked sausage: Simmer about 7oz in the strained soup for 30 minutes, then let infuse off the heat for 30 minutes. Strain to remove the meat, then add a little freshly cooked sliced sausage or diced bacon.

Open ravioli of rabbit with mustard sauce

SERVES 4

5 tbsp butter

1/2 onion, peeled and roughly
    chopped

3 garlic cloves, peeled and cracked

1 thyme sprig

2 bay leaves

1/2 cup white wine

2 back legs of rabbit, skinned

4 cups chicken stock (page 156)

2 tbsp heavy cream

1 tbsp Pommery mustard

1/2 quantity fresh pasta dough
    (page 157) or 16 wonton
    wrappers

salt and pepper

20 tarragon leaves for garnish

to cook the rabbit Preheat the oven to 300°F. Place a small stovetop-to-oven casserole over a low heat. Add 4 tbsp butter and heat until it has melted, then add the onion, garlic, thyme, and bay leaves. Cover and sweat gently until the onion is soft, about 8 minutes. Add the wine and reduce by two-thirds, then add the rabbit legs. Pour in the stock to cover, then put the lid on the casserole. Transfer to the oven and braise until the rabbit meat falls away from the bones easily, about 2 1/2 hours. Let cool for about 30 minutes, then take out the rabbit, reserving the liquid, and strip the meat from the bones. Pull into shreds and put into a bowl.

mustard sauce Strain the cooking liquid into a small pan and bubble to reduce by one-third, then stir in the cream and mustard. Add 2 tsp of this sauce to the meat to keep it moist; set aside.

to cook the wontons or pasta If using pasta, roll it out thinly and cut into 4-inch squares; you will need 16. Add the pasta squares or wonton wrappers to a large pan of boiling salted water and cook until al dente, 1–1 1/2 minutes, then drain.

to finish Meanwhile, whisk the remaining 1 tbsp butter into the sauce, a piece at a time. Put two-thirds of the sauce in a pan over a low heat, stir in the rabbit, and heat through gently; check the seasoning. Warm the remaining sauce in another pan. Place 4 spoonfuls of the hot rabbit mixture in each warmed soup plate, spacing them well apart. Top each mound of rabbit with a wonton wrapper or pasta square. Spoon the remaining mustard sauce all over the ravioli, letting it run through and cover the bottom of the plates. Garnish each ravioli with a tarragon leaf, and serve.

as a main course pie Cook the rabbit, take the meat off the bone, and combine with all of the creamy mustard sauce. Blanch 1 cup shelled fresh peas and a chopped wedge of Savoy cabbage in boiling water for 2 minutes, then drain and combine with the rabbit mixture. Put into a deep 5-cup baking dish. Roll out 8oz puff pastry (about 1/2 package) to make a top crust. Brush the rim of the baking dish with water, cover with the crust, and press to seal. Glaze with beaten egg and bake at 400°F until puffed and golden brown, 25–30 minutes.

Seared veal carpaccio

SERVES 6

1¼lb boneless veal rump, trimmed
salt and pepper
2 tbsp vegetable oil
4 tsp unsalted butter
1 large onion, peeled and roughly
chopped
2 carrots, peeled and roughly
chopped
4–5 thyme sprigs

shallot confit

3 shallots, peeled and minced
7 tbsp extra virgin olive oil

warm mushroom and bean salad

4oz haricots vert (fine green beans)
6oz mixed wild mushrooms, such
as black trumpets and
chanterelles, cleaned
2 tbsp olive oil
1 garlic clove, peeled and cracked
4 tbsp vinaigrette (page 157)

to finish

provolone or Parmesan cheese
shavings
small salad leaves, such as
watercress and arugula

shallot confit   Prepare this first. Put the minced shallots into a small saucepan with a pinch of salt and cover with the olive oil. Place over a very low heat and let the shallots cook slowly in the warm oil until translucent, about 30 minutes. Let cool.

cooking the veal   Preheat the oven to 450°F. Season the veal with salt and pepper. Heat a large, stovetop-to-oven frying pan (with a metal handle) or casserole until hot. Add the vegetable oil and then the butter, and heat. Put the veal into the pan and brown for 2 minutes, then turn to brown on all sides. Remove and set aside. Add the chopped onion, carrots, and thyme sprigs. Return the veal to the pan, placing it on top of the vegetables. Transfer to the oven and roast for 5–6 minutes for medium-rare, or 7–8 minutes for medium, turning the meat over halfway through cooking. Remove and let rest in a warm place for 10 minutes.

warm mushroom and bean salad   Bring a pan of salted water to a boil. Add the green beans and cook until al dente, about 2 minutes. Drain and refresh in a bowl of ice water. Drain, then cut into ³⁄4-inch lengths and set aside. Slice the mushrooms. Heat a large frying pan until hot, then add the olive oil and garlic. Add the mushrooms to the pan and season with salt and pepper. Cook for 1–2 minutes, gently moving the mushrooms around in the pan with a wooden spoon. Tip into a bowl, discarding the garlic.

to finish   Slice the rested veal as thinly as possible across the grain. Add the green beans and shallot confit to the warm mushrooms, along with the vinaigrette. Toss gently to mix and check the seasoning. Arrange the veal slices on large, warmed serving plates, overlapping the slices slightly, and season with salt and pepper. Spoon the mushroom and bean salad on top. Scatter provolone or Parmesan shavings over and garnish with a few small salad leaves. Serve immediately.

as a main course

Double the quantities—you will need a 2½-lb boned and rolled veal loin or rump roast. Cook as above, allowing about 30–40 minutes in the oven. Let rest for 10 minutes. Meanwhile, add a splash of red wine and 1 cup of veal or chicken stock to the pan and stir to deglaze, then strain this jus. Carve the veal into thick slices and serve with the haricots vert and sauté potatoes.

Basics

Chicken stock   MAKES ABOUT 8 CUPS   *2¼lb chicken bones or wings; 1 large onion, peeled and roughly chopped; 1 leek, roughly chopped; 2 celery stalks, roughly chopped; 3 garlic cloves, peeled and cracked; 1 bay leaf; 1 thyme sprig*

Place the chicken bones or wings in a large pot and cover with plenty of cold water, about 10 cups. Bring to a boil and skim, then simmer, skimming frequently, for 20 minutes. Add the onion, leek, celery, garlic, and herbs. Simmer gently for 2 hours, skimming as necessary. Remove from the heat and let cool for 30 minutes. Strain the stock through a cheesecloth-lined sieve into a bowl. Cool, then refrigerate for up to 3 days and use as required.

Fish stock   MAKES ABOUT 6 CUPS   *1¼–1¾lb white fish bones (sole, halibut, etc.), gills removed; 2 tbsp olive oil; ½ fennel bulb, trimmed and roughly chopped; 1 small onion, peeled and chopped; 1 leek (white part only), roughly chopped; 1 celery stalk, roughly chopped; ¼ lemon; 2 parsley sprigs*

Rinse the fish bones under cold running water and set aside. Heat the olive oil in a large, heavy-based pan. Add the vegetables, then cover and sweat gently until soft, 10–15 minutes. Add the fish bones, lemon, and parsley. Pour in 8 cups cold water and bring to a boil, skimming. Lower the heat and simmer gently for 20 minutes, skimming frequently. Remove from the heat and let cool. Strain the stock through a cheesecloth-lined sieve into a bowl. Refrigerate for up to 2 days and use as required.

Vegetable nage   MAKES ABOUT 8 CUPS   *2 onions, peeled; 5 carrots, peeled; 2 celery stalks; 1 leek (white part only); 2 fennel bulbs, trimmed; ½ garlic bulb, halved crosswise; 5 white peppercorns; 3 star anise; 1 tsp fennel seeds; 1–2 sprigs each of chervil, tarragon, dill, and flat-leaf parsley*

Roughly chop all the vegetables and place in a large pot with the garlic and spices. Pour in 8 cups cold water to cover. Bring to a boil over a medium heat, then cover the surface with a piece of parchment paper and lower the heat. Simmer gently for 20 minutes. Remove from the heat and pour the contents of the pot into a bowl. Add the herbs and let cool, then cover with plastic wrap and let infuse in the refrigerator overnight. The next day, strain the nage through a fine sieve into a clean bowl, discarding all the flavorings. Cover and keep in the fridge for up to 3 days and use as required.

Basic short pastry   MAKES 14oz   *1¾ cups all-purpose flour, sifted; ⅛ tsp salt; small pinch of sugar; 10 tbsp unsalted butter, diced; 1 egg, lightly beaten; 1 tbsp milk*

Put the flour, salt, and sugar into a large bowl. Add the diced butter and rub into the flour, using your fingertips, until the mixture looks like fine crumbs. Add the egg and half of the milk, and mix to a dough. Knead lightly until smooth, adding more of the milk if the dough is too dry. Wrap the dough in plastic wrap and let rest in the refrigerator for at least 1 hour before using.

Pasta dough   MAKES 8oz   *1¾ cups "00" pasta flour or 1½ cups all-purpose flour; 2 large eggs; 1 tsp olive oil*

Sift the flour into a food processor. Lightly whisk the eggs and olive oil together in a small bowl. Pour half of the egg mix into the food processor and blend until the mixture resembles fine crumbs, about 1 minute. With the motor running, slowly add the remaining egg mix through the feed tube until you have a smooth, firm dough; you may not need to add all of the egg. Wrap the dough in plastic wrap and let rest in the refrigerator for at least 1 hour before using. When ready to use, roll out the pasta dough, in batches, using a pasta machine. Continue to pass through the machine, narrowing the setting each time, until the pasta sheets are very thin, then cut and cook as required.
note Do not add salt to the dough, as this only will encourage discoloration.

Vinaigrette   MAKES ABOUT 1 CUP   *4 tbsp balsamic vinegar; ⅔ cup extra virgin olive oil; salt and pepper; 3 garlic cloves, peeled and cracked; 1 thyme sprig; 1 rosemary sprig*

Whisk the balsamic vinegar, olive oil, and seasoning together in a bowl. Add the remaining ingredients and transfer to a lidded jar. Let infuse for at least 24 hours, or up to 4–5 days in the refrigerator. Strain and use as required. The vinaigrette can be stored in the fridge for 2–3 weeks.
note To vary the flavor, replace 4 tbsp of the olive oil with walnut oil or hazelnut oil.

Mayonnaise   MAKES ABOUT 2 CUPS   *4 large egg yolks, or 2 tbsp pasteurized egg yolk; 1½ tsp Dijon mustard; ½ tsp salt; ¼ tsp white pepper; 1½ tsp white wine vinegar; 2 cups vegetable or light olive oil*

Put the egg yolks, mustard, salt, pepper, and wine vinegar into a bowl and whisk together. Slowly whisk in the oil, drop by drop to begin with, then in a thin stream, to emulsify. The mayonnaise should be thick and smooth. Check the seasoning. Store in the fridge for up to 3 days.
note If the mayonnaise splits, try this remedy. Put 1 tbsp boiling water into a clean bowl, then slowly whisk in the split mixture—it should re-emulsify. When all the split mixture is incorporated, slowly whisk in the last of the oil.

Pear chutney   MAKES ABOUT 14oz   *⅓ cup packed light brown sugar; ⅓ cup white wine vinegar; 1 bay leaf; ½ tsp mustard seeds; juice of ½ orange; 1 Granny Smith apple, peeled, cored, and grated; 2 star anise; 1 tbsp golden raisins; pinch of salt; 4 ripe pears*

Put all the ingredients, except the pears, into a pot over a medium heat. Bring to a simmer and cook, stirring occasionally, until the mixture has a syrupy consistency, 5–7 minutes. Meanwhile, peel, core, and dice the pears. Add to the pot and cook over a low heat, stirring occasionally, for 10–15 minutes. Check the seasoning and let cool. Store in a jar in the fridge for up to a week.

Index

Acknowledgments

Thank you to David Haman for trying all my recipes at home, and to my girlfriend, Julia, for eating them all! Thanks also to my
staff in the kitchen: Roger, Jason, Marcus, and Anna for helping me with the recipes for photography.